CREATI

# CREATED FOR LOVE

Understanding and Building Self-Esteem

by

John and Agnes Sturt

eagle

Guildford, Surrey

British Library Cataloguing in Publication Data. A
catalogue record for this book is available from the
British Library.

Published by Eagle, and imprint of Inter
Publishing Service (IPS) Ltd. 6-7 Leapale Road,
Guildford, GU1 4JX.

Typeset by the Electronic Book Factory Ltd, Fife,
Scotland.
Printed in the UK by
Caledonian International Book Manufacturing Ltd,
Glasgow.

ISBN: 1 897913 03 6

This book is dedicated to our five children,
their partners and our twelve grandchildren.
Together we are learning to love.

# CONTENTS

# ACKNOWLEDGEMENTS

We wish to acknowledge our indebtedness to many people who have been involved with us in the preparation of this book. Firstly we thank our long-suffering editor, Mrs Joyce Huggett, whose help and wisdom has encouraged us to keep going.

We also greatly appreciate the assistance of many friends who have read the manuscripts and given us valuable feedback and advice. These include Mr Doug Hewlett, Dr John Hitchin, Mrs Shirley Snowdon, Dr Douglas Stewart, Mr Neville Taylor, Mrs Shirley Snowdon.

A number of people have come to us for help in the area of their self-esteem, and have studied various chapters and worked through the exercises. Many others have worked on this material in Self-Esteem Seminars that we have run and have thus helped us shape the content of the book.

We have acknowledged throughout the text and in the Bibliography a number of authors, whose wisdom we have drawn on freely. We very are grateful to Chris Twyman, coming to our aid with his computer skills. Finally, we owe a lot to our publishers for their encouragement and guidance in bringing this book to birth. Writing this book was every bit as challenging as having a baby, though it took longer!

# FOREWORD

The authors of this book will need no introduction to most of their readers in New Zealand. John and Agnes Sturt are well known and well loved, not only in Auckland, where they live, but throughout North and South Island. There, they have earned the affection and appreciation of the countless couples who have attended their many marriage seminars. Others who have never met them personally have been helped and challenged by their broadcasting and speaking ministry.

Readers in England and other parts of the world, however, may not have heard of them. I therefore count it a privilege to introduce there two friends of mine.

I first met John and Agnes in their home in 1990. I felt immediately drawn to them by the warmth of their welcome and their generous, hospitable personalities. Later, I had the privilege of working with them and found myself admiring their rare combination of their gifts: their compassion for hurting people, their faithfulness to biblical truth, their insight into human nature, and their personal desire to go on growing spiritually and emotionally. I felt even further drawn by the ministry of the Christian Counselling Centre they pioneered in Aukland and regretted there was no time to visit this much appreciated haven for the hurting.

My next encounter with the Sturts took place in

England. There, among other things, they worked in the parish of St Nicholas', Nottingham, where my husband was then Rector. Their loving and insightful listening and teaching is still remembered by a wide range of people who attended the seminars they conducted and the meetings at which they spoke. Students and retired people, marrieds and singles alike recall with gratitude John and Anges' sensitivity and humour, concern and care.

It was at a conference for missionaries that I first heard them speak on the subject of self-esteem. 'Why hasn't anyone spoken on this theme before?' was a question which was repeated many times during the week at High Leigh. For many, it was though the Sturts had turned a key in a rusty lock. Now that the door had swung open, many were helped to see why their actions and reactions were less mature and less Christ-like than they would have liked. Better still, they caught a vision of ways in which they could gradually change.

So, when I re-visited Auckland in April 1993, I was delighted to find John and Agnes beavering away at this book. I was touched that they invited me to comment on the material they had produced.

Pockets of insecurity can be found in each of us. These distort our view of ourselves, of others and of God. They sometimes cause us to limp through life. They should also challenge us to go on growing in self-awareness and in grace. This book will help many to discern some of the reasons why they fail to value themselves as highly as God does. It will reveal to others areas of their lives in which growth needs to take place. And it will highlight for yet others ways they may experience an ever-increasing degree of wholeness as they journey through life.

John and Agnes have emphasised in their introduction that some of the exercises they have included
need to be tackled with care. They could put readers
in touch with long-buried painful emotions. When
such feelings or memories surface, wherever possible, these should be shared with a wise and caring
mentor, counsellor or friend. This way they may
well become springboards for the growth that makes
self-awareness productive. These exercises should
also be approached with the humility of mind that
recognises that, though we have a responsibility to
mature in Christ, we can never do this alone. We
need always to remember that God, the generous
Giver, offers us two gifts: his grace, that is, his
undeserved love, and his Spirit. It is my prayer that
readers may open their hands and hearts to receive
both of these gifts. That way this book will not be
just another that they read. Instead, it will become
a tool in the hands of the abundant Giver that will
effect long-lasting and much-needed transformation
of body, mind and spirit.

Joyce Huggett
Cyprus 1994

# INTRODUCTION

Life is a journey towards maturity. Becoming a whole and mature person does not happen automatically. It involves personal effort and growth, intellectually, emotionally and spiritually. This is sometimes painful but always rewarding. Growth to wholeness includes the development of healthy self-esteem. Good self-esteem, or alternatively the lack of it, gives a person either a springboard or a handicap for facing life. As we became aware of our own personal journey and walked with many others for parts of theirs, we decided to find out what are springboards and what are handicaps to good self-esteem.

The well-known author, John Powell, claims that: *"Good self-esteem is the greatest psychological possession you can have."* It is a greater asset than wealth, or success, or even good health. People with good self-esteem can forget about themselves and reach out to others with genuine love and concern. They do not need to prove anything; they know who they are. They do not have to try to fill their emptiness with achievement or material possessions. When they achieve things it is because they believe in what they are doing, not because they are trying to establish their own worth by what they do. They use things and love people. They are concerned with *being rather than doing*.

On the other hand, people with low self-esteem carry around a constant pain inside which produces a self-preoccupation. This makes it difficult for them to forget about themselves. "Many people live lives of quiet desperation."[1] They often seek success or material possessions as a means of establishing their identity and worth. They tend to love things and use people, and find it difficult to form deep relationships. Pleasure-seeking, substance-abuse, a constant search for distraction and workaholism are common substitutes for the missing sense of self worth. A lack of self-esteem makes people want to withdraw from others. They are concerned with *doing rather than being*.

# THE SELF-ESTEEM JOURNEY

The development of self-esteem does not happen instantaneously. It is a journey. This book is based on the belief that good self-esteem is essential for healthy living and meaningful relationships. We know this to be true in our own lives and also in the lives of many others, as we have talked together about their experience. So often the bottom line of people's problems turns out to be a lack of self-worth. But when this issue is addressed and there is a growth in true self-esteem life and relationships change for the better.

Our conviction is that good self-esteem is rooted in a *relationship with God*. The Bible affirms that each of us is of great significance and worth to God. We are created in his image, the objects of his love and of value to him. We must learn to value and love ourselves as he values and loves us. When we discover that we are the objects of God's unconditional love, we can stop feeling worthless. When we discover our true identity in Christ we can start living as children of God. Developing healthy self-esteem is not the most important goal in life – knowing Christ is.[2] But good self-esteem helps us to be who we are and to become what God wants us to become. It helps us in building good relationships with other people and also with God. Growth in our self-esteem is an integral part of life's journey.

This book progresses through a number of stages. In Part 1 we will define good and poor self-esteem. The consequences of low self-esteem are spelt out, as well as the compensating behaviours people often adopt to cover their lack of self-worth. We will then look at how our self-esteem develops and the influences which determine whether a person grows up with a good or poor self-esteem. In Part 2 we suggest steps that can be taken to grow in positive self-esteem.

# A PRACTICAL WORK-BOOK

*Created for Love* is not intended to be a theoretical treatise on self-esteem but a practical manual. Confucius said, many centuries ago: "I hear and I forget, I see and I remember, I do and I understand." So at the end of each chapter there are questions for personal reflection, and specific exercises for those who wish to work on the issues raised in the chapter. Because self-esteem involves our thoughts, feelings and spirits, the exercises are designed to address our minds, emotions and our faith. This "work-book" can be used on your own, or perhaps more effectively in a small-group situation.

Some of these exercises are quite powerful, and

will put you in touch with deep issues and feelings, which may have been buried for many years. So they need to be done with care! It can be painful to have a good look at yourself. "Life is like an onion. You take off one layer at a time, and sometimes you cry!"[3] You may find it helpful to share with a close friend or a counsellor from whom you can receive support. But in any case, *challenge yourself to grow*. You may like to choose exercises initially that you know you can cope with, then return to the harder ones.

We strongly recommend that you keep a *journal*. This can be a small note-book in which you record answers to the questions, insights you obtain and also your feelings as you work through the book. This will become a valuable record of your personal growth journey. It is a very effective way of obtaining perspective on your life. We find it a way of being in touch with what is really going on within us, and above all, of encountering God. A journal provides a mirror on life. "In its pages we may find a moving image which represents who I have been, who I am now, and who I am becoming."[4]

The case histories in this book are about real people, but names and details have been changed to make them unidentifiable. It has been a great privilege to walk with them for a little while on their journey and we are grateful for permission to share their stories. Our lives were enriched as we talked and cried and prayed together. We also acknowledge the help of a number of authors, listed in the Bibliography, who have greatly increased our understanding. But above all, it is in the Bible that we personally discovered our true value and worth. We have found that the Scriptures are full of messages which affirm our uniqueness and significance to God. Many of these have been referred to in this book.

# CREATED FOR LOVE

We have been created *by* love and *for* love. We are designed by God, the source of all love, who loves us individually and wants us to love him. As we respond to his incredible love, we learn to love and value ourselves: learning to love what God loves so much. Also, in response to God's love, we will have the desire to reach out and love others: "We love because he first loved us."[5]

When Jesus said: "I have come that they may have life, and have it to the full",[6] he was not only referring to life after death. He intends us to live life to the full *now*. Jesus also told us: "Then you will know the truth, and the truth will set you free."[7]

This is a most profound statement. "The truth" is not only truth about salvation, but ALL truth. Truth liberates us from bondage of all kinds. When we get in touch with the truth about ourselves and do not run away from it, we can be set free from a self-imposed prison. Sometimes the truth hurts, but painful things in our lives often produce the most growth in our character.[8]

Writing a book together has been challenging, rewarding and difficult. Our aim has been to present both a feminine and masculine perspective on self-esteem. It is our sincere prayer that God will use this book to enrich the lives of others struggling with the development of their identity and self-worth. We invite you to share this journey together with us.

John and Agnes Sturt
Auckland, New Zealand.

# PART 1

# UNDERSTANDING SELF-ESTEEM

The purpose of Part 1 is to provide an understanding of self-esteem, in the following way:

**Chapter 1** defines good self-esteem. People with good self-esteem are comfortable with themselves and with others. We believe that a loving relationship with God through Christ is ultimately the way to discover our true value and worth.

**Chapter 2** looks at poor self-esteem and how this follows negative messages about ourselves that we received in childhood. These are reinforced by our negative internal dialogue, or self-talk. Eventually, we may develop distorted thought patterns which become a permanent mindset, which can then be hardened by negative cyclical thinking.

**Chapter 3** explores the early development of our self-concept, starting with pre-birth factors. We then point to some of the positive influences leading to a good self-esteem and also the negative ones that result in a poor self-image. The self-concept that we finish up with is the result of these influences plus the choices we make in response to them.

**Chapter 4** outlines some of the consequences of a low self-esteem. Common compensating behaviours for low self-esteem, or defence mechanisms, are described. Low self-esteem can also contribute to long-term emotional states, such as stress and depression. It also has a significant bearing on our relationships both with people and with God.

**Chapter 5** attempts to define a theology of self-esteem, Firstly, we examine the "man is muck" theology, which has been prevalent in some church teaching for many centuries. Then we look at a positive biblical basis for a healthy self-esteem.

All of us struggle to some extent with our self-image. This section lays a foundation for understanding self-esteem in preparation for Part 2 of the book, which describes ways to grow in our self-esteem.

# ONE

# GOOD SELF-ESTEEM

*We are not what we think we are,*
*but what we think, we are.*

Anonymous

Steven is a top commercial pilot at the peak of his career. But just when he expected life to be rich and fulfilling, his marriage of twenty years came to an end. Steven was full of questions: "What went wrong?" "How is it I can fly an aeroplane without any trouble but prang my marriage"? "Why am I successful in most things I want to do but can't relate to people?" "I've met a wonderful lady, but am afraid to risk another relationship."

We spent some time reflecting on his childhood. Steven was the youngest of three children. His older brother suffered from quite severe asthma and was the focus of his parents' attention for many years. His sister coped with this by being naughty and received plenty of attention that way! Steven chose a third route – being good. He was very compliant and could always be relied upon to do what he was told. His mother often boasted that they could leave him for hours to play happily with his toys in a corner.

Steven does not remember his parents ever praising or affirming him for anything. It was always assumed that he would do the right thing. He did very well at school, hoping for the approval of his parents, but never receiving any. So he tried harder, and achieved everything he set his mind to. He became a perfectionist, setting very high standards for himself and also for others. But when others did not meet his standards Steven was quick to let them know about it. He was aware of being very critical of others and angry if they disappointed him. He was also sensitive to and shattered by any criticism of himself. It was not hard for him to understand why his wife found him difficult to live with!

"But what can I do about it?" asked Steven. "How can I change?"

We discussed the issue of his self-esteem. Steven saw that his sense of self-worth was based entirely on achievement. He knew that he was competent but never felt that anyone loved or appreciated him. Over the next few weeks he thought through his basic value system. He was a Christian, but had not grasped that God accepted him and loved him unconditionally, without him having to earn it. He discovered that his true value and worth depended on who he was, not on what he achieved. Steven started to love himself, and this freed him to forget about himself. Now he was able to reach out to others in a new way, and meet their needs. All his relationships began to improve.

*Steven's journey is the theme of this book.*


# WHAT IS GOOD SELF-ESTEEM?

Our self-concept includes both our self-image and self-esteem. It starts in our minds, where at a subconscious level our *self-image*, (what we *think* about ourselves) is formed from a very early age. This in turn affects us at an emotional level (how we *feel* about ourselves) which is essentially our self-esteem. Our self-esteem, or sense of self-worth, always includes a value judgement of ourselves. This results in our feeling well about ourselves or feeling badly about ourselves. Our self-esteem determines much of our behaviour, including how we relate to other people.

Three thousand years ago a very wise man said, "As [a man] thinketh in his heart, so is he".[1] Clearly, we do not think with our hearts but with our minds. But to the Hebrews, the "heart" is the innermost being, the centre of reflection. Solomon is stating that what we think about ourselves must be consistent with what we feel deep down inside ourselves. My "nut" and my "gut" must synchronise; my self-image must match up with my self-esteem. What we think and feel about ourselves must be in harmony.

If my self-image and my self-esteem are not in harmony, there will be constant tension and internal discomfort. When my mind and heart combine in a negative self-concept, I will be locked into low self-esteem. This will result in a measure of internal consistency but it is a destructive and unpleasant way to live. On the other hand, if my mind and heart are united in a positive self-concept, I will have a good self-esteem. I will be free from internal tension and enabled to live in a healthy way. I will feel good about myself and others. Unfortunately, this experience is rare. Many people, even Christians, do not feel a sense of self-worth. People with healthy self-esteem can say, and really mean it: "It's good to be me!" "I know I'm not perfect and have a lot of growing to do, but I'm happy with who I am." "The Lord hasn't finished with me yet, but he is still working on me."[2] "The more you get to know me, the more you'll like me!"

You can recognise people with good self-esteem by the following general characteristics:

## *They are comfortable with themselves*

They accept themselves, "warts and all". This will not stop them from working on their shortcomings and failings. In fact, the reality of this acceptance frees them to make changes. People with a strong self-esteem have a balanced view of themselves, neither underestimating nor overestimating their abilities.[3] They have a tolerant attitude towards themselves which helps to prevent them developing false guilt.[4] A good self-esteem enables people to be in touch with their emotions, such as fear, anger, love, jealousy, worry. They can acknowledge their feelings, but are not bowled over by them; feel them, but are not wiped out by them. They can take life's disappointments in their stride.

Jillian's story is an example of how a good self-esteem can enable a person to cope with terrible circumstances, and even to grow through them. From the start she experienced a lot of violence in her marriage, but she persisted with the relationship for twelve years. Eventually, she left Sam to ensure the safety of her two daughters and herself. In talking with Jillian, we were amazed that she was free of bitterness. She still had a real concern for her ex-husband. Although she had lost respect for him, she refused to blame him and spoke well of him to her children. She reflected: "Our marriage hasn't worked out, but I'm determined to make a life for myself and for the girls." Jillian's essentially healthy self-esteem was never shaken, and has been a major factor enabling her to survive the trauma of the past few years. She did not allow her experiences to stop her thinking positively and acting responsibly.

An important part of healthy living is *taking responsibility* for *our own lives* and not blaming others for our feelings and problems. This ability indicates good self-esteem in people. They feel able to deal with most situations that come their way. When tragedy enters their lives, they are less likely to ask: "Why has this happened to me?" Rather, the question in their minds is: "Lord, what do you want to teach me through this?" They are open to change and growth.

People with good self-esteem *find satisfaction in simple everyday pleasures*. They do not need repeated "highs" for life to seem worthwhile. They appreciate the world around them and value the little things: a tiny flower blooming in an unexpected place; a smile from a stranger; a shaft of sunlight after the rain; the feeling of refreshment after a night's rest.

People with healthy self-esteem *enjoy their own company*. This does not mean they do not like being with other people when possible. But if you like yourself, you will have good company twenty-four hours a day! Times of aloneness and silence can be very precious, providing opportunity for rest and renewal away from the bustle and noise of a busy lifestyle. These occasions present opportunities for reflection; a chance to know oneself at a deeper level, or perhaps to listen to God.[5] But if people do not really like themselves, being alone can be very threatening. They will usually try to fill the silence by turning on the radio or TV or finding some other form of escape.

*Being able to laugh at yourself* is a mark of a

person with good self esteem. I (Agnes), grew up in a family with brothers who liked to tease, and I was slow to develop this ability to laugh at myself. I found it hard to take a joke that was directed against me, even when it was in fun and without malice. It has taken me a long time to learn to see myself objectively, and to believe that people could be laughing with me, rather than at me.

Many people can laugh at others, but find it threatening to be in an embarrassing situation or the focus of amusement themselves. We should "take ourselves seriously but not too solemnly".[6] An old Chinese proverb says: "Blessed is he who can laugh at himself, for he shall never cease to be amused!"

## *They are comfortable with others*

The way we feel about others is usually the consequence of the way we feel about ourselves. "We do not see things as they are, we see them as *we are*."[7] People with healthy self-esteem feel good about themselves and in turn, feel good about others. The Bible states eight times over, and Jesus commands us to: *"Love your neighbour AS yourself"* (emphasis ours).[8] This principle will be developed in more detail later.

People with good self-esteem usually *expect to like and trust others* and assume that others will like and trust them. Of course, as we grow up we learn to be discriminating when we discover that some people do not have our best interests at heart, and in fact may want to harm us. But the development of this basic trust,[9] which depends largely on the kind of relationship we have with our parents, is integral to the development of good self-esteem.

People who have a good self-esteem *feel positively*

*about others*. They are able to love others and consider their interests.[10] They will have personal relationships that are lasting and satisfying, based on mutual sharing and self-revelation. Without a sense of self-worth I will not feel good about myself, and if I do not like what I feel inside I will certainly not want to reveal myself to you. Hence, I would find it difficult to cope with the vulnerability that intimacy entails and the possible rejection that may follow. "If I show you who I am and you don't like me, that's all I've got."[11] Low self-esteem is one of the factors that makes it difficult for married couples to really enjoy a close relationship. But people with good self-esteem can be open and intimate and encourage each other's growth.[12]

A strong self-esteem helps people to develop *a sense of responsibility towards others*. They will be more likely to see someone else's need and respond in some way. They will neither push people around nor allow themselves to be pushed around. Feeling badly about ourselves leads to an irresponsible attitude towards others. It was Cain's hurt pride and refusal to admit his mistake that led to the attitude: "Am I my brother's keeper?", and eventually to murdering Abel.[13]

Another quality essential for good relationships is *respect*. David Beckett was a young teacher at the boarding school that I (John) attended. He had a quality about him that encouraged our respect. He showed genuine interest in each of us, greeting us by name if we passed in the corridor or playground. He made time for us when we went to him with a problem. I always felt better after being with him. As I look back to David, and a few other people I have met like him, I begin to understand what G.K. Chesterton meant when he said: "The really great

person is one who makes everyone else feel great."
The respect and care David showed for us reflected
how he felt about himself.

People with healthy self-esteem are more likely to
respect and *accept the differences* they see in other
people. If I have a good self-esteem, your differences
will interest and attract me. But if I do not really
like who I am, your differences will threaten me
and I will find it hard to accept you. The more
threatened people are by differences in others, the
more aggressive they are likely to become. It can
even lead to an urge to kill people who are different,
or at least to ostracise them.

Good self-esteem is an essential factor for healthy
living. It enables people *to be at peace within themselves and at peace with others*. Solomon said: "A
heart at peace gives life to the body, but envy rots
the bones."[14] When we are at peace with ourselves
we can be at peace with the world. Peacefulness is
a characteristic of people with good self-esteem.


# SELF-ESTEEM AND THE CHRISTIAN FAITH

It is our conviction that we are not fully mature
until we have a true relationship with God. A person
without God is less than human. It is the life of
God within us that makes us fully human and fully
alive.[15] St Irenaeus, in the second century, said:
"The glory of God is a human being who is fully
alive." True self-worth starts with an awareness of
being *"created in the image of God"*,[16] and of being
of great value and worth to him.

Francis Schaeffer put it like this:

For twentieth-century man, this phrase "the image of God" is as important as anything in Scripture, because men today can no longer answer that crucial question, "Who am I?" In his own naturalistic theories, with the uniformity of cause and effect in a closed system with an evolutionary concept of a mechanical, a chance parade from atom to man, man has lost his unique identity ... In contrast, I stand in the flow of history. I know my origin ... I see my origin in Adam and in God creating man in his own image.[17]

The image of God in us was spoiled by sin, but not removed. The good news is that by faith it is possible to be re-created in the likeness of Christ, and to be adopted into God's family. Our worth is enhanced further when we realise that each of us has been given a specific life-task to do. St Paul summed it up in one magnificent statement: "We are God's workmanship, created in Christ Jesus to do good works, which God prepared in advance for us to do."[18]

Many people lack this positive view of themselves. They may have had destructive childhood experiences which have left them with a poor self-concept, and these issues have never been dealt with. They have accepted salvation by faith, but their minds have not been "renewed" yet,[19] and old thought patterns have not been changed. They have not grasped the extent of the unconditional love of God, which accepts us all just as we are, accepting the sinner, though not the sin. God's love can transform the way we feel about ourselves. As we experience the warmth of God's love in our lives, past hurts can be healed. We can then discover and enjoy the freedom of being children of God.

This happened to Michael, who grew up in a home where he was never affirmed or praised. In fact, his father went out of his way to criticise and devalue everything he did. When he became a Christian, his father rejected him totally. But as Michael grew in his faith, he discovered a new identity in Christ. He realised he did have value and worth. He grew in self-esteem and confidence. He also came to see his father in a different light, someone who had been hurt in his own childhood. Michael started to reach out to him with care and concern, attempting to restore their relationship.

Good self-esteem can be summed up simply: an awareness that I am both

| CAPABLE | and | LOVABLE |

We all need to know that *we are reasonably competent* and able to handle most situations that come our way. This does not mean convincing myself or others that "I'm the greatest", in Mohammed Ali style. But it does mean becoming aware of the abilities God has given me, and being ready to face the world with his help.

But in addition, I need to know and feel deep within me that *I am lovable*. This is a message I should receive from my parents and significant people in my life as I grow up. I must also be convinced of God's unconditional love for me; that he not only loves me but that I am lovable to him. Many people give intellectual assent to this, but they do not *feel* loved by God. Only about forty centimetres separates our brains and our hearts, but this is the longest journey we all have to make! Head and heart must agree about this matter; thoughts and feelings must be in harmony. Like a good photograph, my self-picture should neither flatter nor distort but truly represent who I am.

Knowing that I am capable and lovable is like the two sides of the golden coin of self-esteem. So many people who do not feel lovable spend their lives trying to prove that they are capable, hoping that one day someone will really love them. But it does not work that way! This message of being both capable and lovable must be communicated to children if they are to grow up with a sense of good self-esteem.

## SUMMARY

Good self-esteem means being at peace with ourselves and with others. Because we accept and respect ourselves we can treat others that way too. People with good self-esteem take responsibility for their own lives and personal growth, but they also have a desire to care for others. They feel both capable and lovable.

# REFLECTIONS AND EXERCISES

1 *Start your journal.* Head up one page with the words I AM ... Then write down all the things you can think of that you are:

e.g.  a woman/man    an only child    Chinese/European/Indian
      Short/tall         dark/fair        plump/thin
      reserved         friendly         thoughtful
      a wife/husband   a mother/father  middle-aged, etc.

- For how many of these can you say: "I'm pleased about that"? Can you say with conviction: "It's good to be me!"?[20]

2 If you are in a group situation, form pairs, and one of you ask the other: "Who are you?". Keep asking the question until your partner runs out of answers. Then change over and repeat the exercise.

- Think about the answers you have given. Do they really represent who you are? How hard was it to keep answering this question?

3 Make a list in your journal of ten or more adjectives that describe you, e.g. you are: caring, confident, hasty, practical, outgoing, honest, hardworking ...

- Ask a close friend to write a similar list about you.
- Compare the two lists. What can you learn from this exercise about how you see yourself and how others see you?

4 Think of the last time you were angry, disappointed, lonely, discouraged or uncertain.

- To what extent are you able to take responsibility for your life, emotions and actions?
- Do you tend to blame others for your feelings?

5 Remember the last few times when you have been alone, e.g. came home to an empty house; found yourself alone for a while, waiting for a friend to turn up.

- How did you fill in the silence?
- To what degree do you enjoy times of aloneness?
- To what extent does your comfort/discomfort with times of aloneness reflect how you feel about yourself?

6 How do you feel when you are in a new group? How long does it take you to feel part of a group? Do you have the feeling that everyone else belongs, or "is in the know", except you?

- What helps you to feel part of a group? When joining a new group how do you attempt to "get on board"?
- If you are in a group situation now, discuss how it was for you when you first joined this group, and how you feel now.

7 Do people really respect each other in your family, your workplace, your church, your community?

- Are you part of the answer or part of the problem?
- Which people do you find it hard to respect, and why?

8 Reflect on Ephesians 2:10.

- What does it mean to you to know that you are "God's workmanship", i.e. created in God's likeness?
- As a Christian, you have been "created in Christ". To what extent is Christ's likeness being formed in you? (See Eph 4:13.)
- God has "prepared in advance" significant tasks for each of us to do. What "good works" are you doing for him?

9 Spend some time thinking about or discussing God's amazing unconditional love for us.

- Read 1 Corinthians 13:4–7 as a description of the way God loves us, as well as the way we should love others.

10 Say out loud to at least one friend, and if possible to five or six people on separate occasions: "I like being me, and the more you get to know me, the more you will like me!".

- What effect did this exercise have on you? What does your response to this exercise say about you?
- Reflect on the variety of responses you received from your friends. What do you think their replies said about them?

11 Would you choose yourself for a close friend? If so, write down in your journal as many reasons as you can think of for liking yourself as a friend.

- Share this in your group. They will probably think of some good reasons you have omitted!

# TWO

# POOR SELF-ESTEEM

*Of all our infirmities, the most savage
is to despise our being.*

Montaigne, 1533–1592

Poor self-esteem is easier to experience than to define. Essentially it means to feel badly about yourself, see yourself as inferior, insignificant and of little worth. People with low self-esteem usually think negatively about themselves, other people, the world and God. Sometimes they even hate themselves. They find it very difficult to make lasting relationships. The negative thoughts they have about themselves lead to negative feelings. This often results in self-destructive behaviour, such as overeating, drug abuse, promiscuity, and even suicide.

Julie was an attractive young lady of twenty-four, smartly dressed and well-groomed. She was also a very successful student, halfway through her second degree at university. She stood hesitantly at the door until I (John) invited her a second time to come in and take a seat. Julie had just been discharged from a psychiatric hospital where she was admitted following a suicide attempt. I could not help wondering why such a good looking and successful young person would try to end her life.

Perhaps she had just gone through a very traumatic experience.

So I said, "Julie, I know you were told to have some counselling, and it's not easy to talk to a stranger. I think you're courageous to even come today, and I'd really like to help if I can." After a moment's silence she said, "There's not much to talk about really. I don't know what went wrong . . . or why I slashed my wrists . . . but life seems so pointless . . . it's not worth living . . . I don't think you can help me."

We explored a variety of avenues. Her studies were going well and she enjoyed academic work. In fact she thought this was the only part of her life that was any good. She did not have financial difficulties and lived with some compatible flat-mates. I asked if she had experienced a relationship break-up, but she said: "That's not likely. I've never had any close friends. No one would ever be interested in me, I'm so boring."

This was genuinely what she thought of herself, and she could not see herself in any other light. We started to talk about her childhood. She had been brought up in a very comfortable home and had always been given everything she needed. Her brother and sister had done well professionally and she was constantly encouraged to achieve like they had. She was a good pianist. When friends visited, her mother would ask her to play in front of the visitors.

Her parents were very proud of her until she reached her mid-teens, when she developed some ideas of her own, with which they disagreed. But she only felt loved and valued by them when she was achieving the things they wanted her to do and agreeing with their ideas. Unfortunately, however hard she tried, it was never good enough. She never succeeded in fully pleasing them and she never felt loved for herself. "I suppose they loved me, but I can't remember them ever telling me. They seldom had time for me. If ever I wanted to talk about what was important to me it would end up with a lecture from Dad."

Like Julie, so many people have only received *conditional love* from parents and other significant people. For them, love and acceptance have to be deserved; their worth and value have to be proved; their right to be alive is only justified by what they achieve or produce. This kind of thinking makes it difficult for anybody to accept God's unconditional love. If human approval has to be earned, it is logical to think we must earn God's favour as well.[1]

## OUR INTERNAL DIALOGUE

We are constantly being influenced by our "self-talk" or the internal dialogue that goes on all the time in our minds. Sometimes we are aware of it, but most of the time we are not. However, this dialogue determines many of our attitudes and affects our behaviour. Messages that we pick up in childhood become imprinted on our brains, like tape recordings, so that every time we experience a similar situation the "tape" switches on.[2] It is very easy to respond automatically to these messages. But, hard though it is, it is possible to challenge them and in fact to change them, erasing the old "tapes" and creating new ones. (This process of dealing with our internal dialogue is more fully described in Chapter 6.)

Bob grew up in a home where his father had very rigid ideas and ruled the family harshly and

was suspicious of everyone and always suspected
ulterior motives in people. He never trusted Bob
and constantly checked up on him to see that he
had done what was expected of him. He often told
Bob he was unreliable. Consequently, Bob grew
up unable to trust anyone, had no confidence in
himself and, in fact, became an unreliable person.
Not surprisingly, Bob thought of God as an ogre who
could not be trusted and who demanded retribution
without mercy or forgiveness.

The messages we pick up from others and the conclusions we draw about ourselves, life and God may
not be accurate. The inferences we draw from what
we hear may not represent the intentions behind
other people's words. Bob's father probably sincerely
thought he was doing the best for his family, warning
them of the hard world out there and trying to instil
a sense of responsibility. His harsh treatment of Bob
reflected his own rigid upbringing.

We can also reach negative conclusions about
ourselves merely from a lack of positive messages,
like Alice did. Alice's parents were very caring but
shy and reserved. As a child she was compliant
and always did what she was told. She was a good
student and did well at most things she applied
herself to. But Alice was never affirmed for her
behaviour or for what she achieved. It was just
expected of her. The only occasion she can remember her mother praising her was when she won a
scholarship to university. When her mother started
to congratulate her, her father broke in, saying,
"Stop! You'll give her a swelled head. She has a
lot of hard study to do yet" Alice grew up believing
that she was never quite good enough and, in fact,
a failure.

Children seldom reveal to others what is going

on in their minds. They are unable to evaluate it objectively and unless the adults in their lives are very perceptive and sensitive, they may never get a chance to talk about it openly or correct misconceptions that have formed. Later on, negative thinking can develop into distorted patterns of thinking. Seriously distorted thinking is a characteristic of mental illness.

Even normal people carry around distorted perceptions of one kind or another. Unfortunately, these can develop into habitual patterns of faulty thinking. The task of the therapist is to help clients understand any illogical flaws in their world-view and readjust these.[3] Effective counselling is more concerned with this process than "fixing" problems.

Cognitive Behaviour therapists affirm that what goes on in our *minds* affects our *behaviour*; also that desired behaviour may result from cognitive change. Our thinking affects our emotions, behaviour and even our physical health. Secular psychology fails to acknowledge the reality of sin and its damaging effect on our minds. To ensure permanent changes in our lives, it is necessary to receive God's forgiveness. We must also forgive those whose sins against us have left us hurt, angry, fearful, insecure and doubting our self-worth. We are then able to pray for the power of the Holy Spirit to help us change our thinking and behaviour.

Albert Ellis, the founder of Rational-Emotive Therapy, stated: "At the heart of psychological disturbance lies the tendency of humans to make devout, absolutistic evaluations of the perceived events in their lives. These evaluations are couched in the form of dogmatic 'musts', 'shoulds', 'have tos' and 'oughts'."[4] The following is a summary of some of the most damaging thinking distortions.[5]

# SOME COMMON DISTORTED THOUGHT PATTERNS

## *Black-and-white thinking*

This means thinking rigidly in extremes, or polarising your thinking:

> "I lost my temper, therefore I'm a bad person."
> "I failed the last test . . . I'll never succeed."
> "I forgot again . . . I'm a dummy."
> "I'm a sinner . . . therefore I'm worthless."

## *Self-labelling*

This is an extension of rigid thinking in which I put myself in a box. It is like wearing a T-shirt message which tells the world what I feel about myself, e.g: "I'm a born loser"; "I'm stupid"; "I'm ugly; "I'm not very strong"; "I'm not worth much". Some people behave as if they had a message like that on the front of their T-shirts, and on the back: "Please kick me!"

## *Viewing the world through dark glasses*

This means filtering reality, usually disregarding the positive and seeing everything negatively: e.g. "I'm just a housewife. I guess I can cook and run a home, but that's not much"; "I'm overweight . . . no one would be interested in me"; "I'm not very clever . . . I'd look silly attempting that . . . so I'd better not try"; "It's not worth praying . . . God wouldn't listen to me."

## *Grasshopper thinking or kangaroo jumping*

This means jumping to conclusions and interpreting all events as if they apply to me. A person with low self-esteem will choose negative deductions most often. For example:

"He didn't ring me ... he doesn't care about me."

"She looks upset ... I've done something wrong."

"He doesn't know how I feel ... he doesn't love me."

"They are laughing at me ... they must despise me."

## Telescopic vision

We can look through a telescope from either end. When viewing *weaknesses*, it is as if I use the telescope in the normal way, blowing up little mistakes out of all proportion, e.g. "I can't remember names ... I must be stupid."; "I forgot to introduce him ... I'm bad hostess."; "I didn't thank her ... I'm an ungrateful person."

If I turn the telescope around the other way to view my *strengths*, they will appear insignificant, e.g: "I completed the training, but that's nothing; anyone could have done that." "I cooked a nice meal, but nobody thanked me for it, so it probably wasn't much good."

## The slave-driver mentality

Many people not only become slaves to early messages they picked up, but they crack the whip on themselves. This is known as "the tyranny of the shoulds". Here are some examples of common heavy injunctions, expressed both positively and negatively:

"I *should* have done better."      "I *should not* be weak."

| | |
|---|---|
| "I *must* please every-one." | "I *shouldn't* take any time off." |
| "I *ought* to be perfect." | "I *ought not* to feel hurt." |
| "I *must* be strong all the time." | "I *must not* feel tired." |
| "I *have to* hurry." | "I *must not* waste time." |

These are very powerful messages which can become a permanent mindset and an intolerable burden, leading to false guilt. Dr Frank Lake called this process the "hardening of the oughteries"! These messages need to be challenged and evaluated, but many people have incorporated some of these injunctions firmly into their value system and these are very hard to change. Ways of doing this are described in Chapter 6.[6] Confucius said: "Everything has its beauty, but not everyone sees it." People with low self-esteem not only have problems in seeing beauty in others, but usually fail to see it in themselves. This leads to a process of cyclical thinking.

## CYCLICAL THINKING

Negative thinking can go round and round in our minds in a vicious circle, reinforcing itself over and over again, shown as in Figure 1.

If this destructive cycle is not challenged and changed, a person's self-esteem continues to deteriorate and this will affect their whole life in the following way.

*THINKING . . . FEELING . . . ACTING*

What we think about ourselves affects what we feel about ourselves and this determines how we

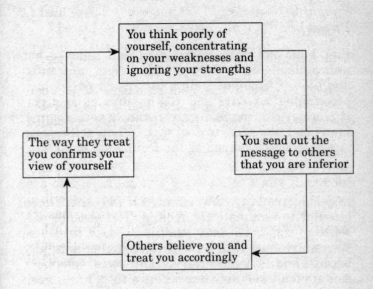

**Figure 1.** The Low Self-Esteem Cycle

treat ourselves. Low self-esteem progresses in a downward spiral. It starts with negative thinking and destructive attitudes, which produce negative feelings. These, in turn, lead to negative behaviours. The sequence can be something like this:

## I THINK

That people would not like me if they knew the real me. I see myself as ugly and unattractive, particularly to members of the opposite sex. I wonder why others can always do things better than I can and have more ability than I do. It is as if everyone has the secret to life except me. As someone put it: "All the world has been invited to a party and I've been left out!"

*I FEEL*

that I am not only incompetent and unloved but unlovable. I feel a failure and useless, unwanted and alone.[7] This gut feeling becomes a pain which preoccupies my days and fills my dreams at night. It is a devastating feeling, constantly accusing me. I may feel powerless to deal with it. Low self-esteem has been aptly defined as the feeling of *shame*.[8]

*I ACT*

in destructive ways towards myself and others in an attempt to eliminate the feeling. The absence of a sense of self-worth may lead me to such things as substance abuse to dull the pain; sexual promiscuity because I do not value my body; anti-social behaviour as I am not likely to value others either. I may even be convinced there is no point in living any more and I would be better off dead, as was the case with Julie.

Julie eventually came to grips with the issue of her incredibly poor self-esteem, and made some significant changes to the way she thought and felt about herself. She began to understand why she had tried to end her life, when in reality she had many excellent qualities and gifts. She realised that she could not make her parents love her unconditionally, and that they really did not know how to love this way. Her parents depended on their own and their children's achievements for their sense of self-worth and had no concept of valuing themselves for just being. So they were only able to love Julie for what she did, not for what she was.

In discovering that they were needy people too, Julie was able to start reaching out to them, trying to bridge the gap that had developed between them over the years. When I last saw her, she was still working on her self-esteem and confidence, but assured me that she did not think she would ever attempt to end her life again.

## SUMMARY

A battered self-esteem is something we all have to deal with in some degree or another. We have all been hurt as well as having hurt others; we have all been sinned against as well as having sinned. Many people are emotionally crippled by the view they have of themselves. The powerful effect of negative messages received in childhood, reinforced by negative self-talk, prevents them from personal fulfilment in life. It not only stunts personal growth but inhibits relationships. But this can be changed, with God's help and a determination to be different.

# REFLECTIONS AND EXERCISES

1 *Reflect on your childhood.* What positive influences can you think of which helped build your self-esteem. Write them down in your journal. Also, identify messages you received while growing up which may have undermined your self-esteem.

   NOTE. This is an awareness exercise, *not* an opportunity to apportion blame. Parents usually do the best they can for their children, within the limits of their own experience and knowledge.

2 Go back in memory to your childhood, and see yourself aged six or seven. Go into the living room of your old family home. Sit down and relax. Spend some time getting used to the old familiar surroundings. See your father come into the room. What are you feeling when you see him? What does he say or do? What do you say or do? Repeat the process with your mother coming in.

   • What feelings are you left with? How do you feel about yourself as the child?
     – If you have positive feelings, thank God for them.
     – If you have negative feelings, ask God to help you understand them and deal with them.
   • If you are in a safe group, share as much as you want to with the others. (Do not interrupt anyone's story, or try to analyse their experience for them.)
   • At the end of this exercise, spend some time praying for one another.

3 How much of your behaviour and activities do you think are directed towards proving your worth or trying to become acceptable to others? Record your thoughts about this in your journal.

4 Identify some of the "self-talk" that has gone on in your mind today.

- Has it been positive or unhelpful?
- Have you found yourself in a negative cycle of thinking?
- Discuss this in your group.

5 Try to identify some of the "taped messages" that play repeatedly in your mind. Here are some examples, but there are many more:

"I must try to please everybody, or they won't like me."
"Don't show your feelings, it's a sign of weakness."
"Time is precious. Don't waste a minute!"
"You'll probably fail."
"If I'm not completely successful in all I do, I'm a failure."
"I must solve other people's problems to be a caring person."
"I must keep the peace in all my relationships, or else my world will fall apart."

- Record any messages in your journal that come to mind.
- Do you want to change any of them?
- Your group members may be able to help you explore ways to make changes. (A process of changing these distorted messages is outlined in Chapter 6.)

6 Look through the section on "Distorted Thought Patterns" (pp. 24–26).

  • Can you identify examples of these in your own thinking?

7 Think about any one-word labels you may have applied to yourself in the past, or even some you may be wearing now. For example:

Dummy    Wise-guy      Helpless   Strong
Rescuer  Martyr        Clown      Sophisticated
Cool     Fitness-freak Superior   Smart . . . etc.

  • Reflect on why you might have chosen a particular label, what purpose it serves, and whether you still need to wear it.
  • If you are in a group situation, in which sufficient trust has developed, share some of your findings about your "labels". Check out the perceptions you have of yourself with the others.
  • How hard would it be to let go of these labels? What would help you to deal with them properly?

8 How do you view your own strengths and weaknesses? I.e., which way do you usually hold the "telescope"? Do you tend to magnify your weaknesses and minimise your strengths, or can you see both realistically?

9 Try to make the connection between something that you *thought* about yourself today and some *feeling* you experienced. Write it down. Our thoughts determine most of our feelings and the resultant feeling depends on our value system or "world view".

- It would be helpful to discuss this as a group activity.

10 Do the evaluation of your self-esteem set out on the next page. This is not an absolute measure, but a useful indication of the degree to which you need to work on this issue. Your score depends a little on how you are feeling at the time, and maybe on the weather! But on the whole it is a reliable reflection of how you feel about yourself. (This test is a modification of a similar one prepared by John Powell.)

Read note (9) in the References and Notes section AFTER completing the assessment.

- If you are in a group, discuss the questionnaire afterwards in twos or threes.
- It would be enlightening to do this assessment again in a few months' time to see how you may have changed.

# HOW YOU SEE YOURSELF
## Date (1)...........(2)...........

INSTRUCTIONS Fill in the date. Each of the twenty five statements below is concerned with your self-esteem. Each can be answered by using one of the five words at the top of the columns. Make your choice, then put the number that is indicated below the word in the box alongside the question you are working on. For example, if your answer is "SOMETIMES", put a 3 in the third box along the line, and so on. Do not spend too long deliberating on your answers. Your initial (gut) reaction is probably the right one! After answering all the questions, add up the numbers in each column and total them.

**Note**: There is no "pass" or "fail" score. This test is just to help identify if you have a problem in this area that you should be working on.

It would be helpful to discuss this test with a close friend or person whose opinion you trust, especially questions you found difficult to answer.

Keep this test and do it again in 6–12 months time to see if there has been any change.

When you have completed this questionnaire, see Note 9 in the references.

| | ALWAYS | MOST TIMES | SOMETIMES | SELDOM | NEVER |
|---|---|---|---|---|---|
| | 1 | 2 | 3 | 4 | 5 |
| Do you like yourself? | | | | | |
| Do you think others like you? | | | | | |
| Are you intellectually capable? | | | | | |
| Do you express your feelings openly? | | | | | |
| Are you successful in what you do? | | | | | |
| Do you see yourself as an attractive person? | | | | | |
| Is comparing yourself with others unprofitable? | | | | | |
| Can you accept compliments? | | | | | |
| Are you comfortable in complimenting others? | | | | | |
| Do you enjoy your work? | | | | | |
| Do you think of yourself as a loving person | | | | | |
| Do you feel loved by God? | | | | | |
| Do you enjoy meeting and talking to people? | | | | | |
| Are you satisfied with your present life situation? | | | | | |
| Are you pleased to be you? | | | | | |
| Do you respect yourself? | | | | | |
| Do you take care of your own needs? | | | | | |
| Do you have a balanced life (rest, work, play, etc)? | | | | | |
| Do you enjoy time on your own? | | | | | |
| Do you trust others? | | | | | |
| Do you see yourself as a confident person? | | | | | |
| Do you feel in control of your life? | | | | | |
| Are you considerate of others? | | | | | |
| Do you contribute positively to the lives of others? | | | | | |
| Do you enjoy a relationship with God? | | | | | |
| SUB-TOTAL | | | | | |
| TOTAL | | | | | |

We suggest that you do this test a second time
after working through the book.

| | ALWAYS | MOST TIMES | SOMETIMES | SELDOM | NEVER |
|---|---|---|---|---|---|
| | 1 | 2 | 3 | 4 | 5 |
| Do you like yourself? | | | | | |
| Do you think others like you? | | | | | |
| Are you intellectually capable? | | | | | |
| Do you express your feelings openly? | | | | | |
| Are you successful in what you do? | | | | | |
| Do you see yourself as an attractive person? | | | | | |
| Is comparing yourself with others unprofitable? | | | | | |
| Can you accept compliments? | | | | | |
| Are you comfortable in complimenting others? | | | | | |
| Do you enjoy your work? | | | | | |
| Do you think of yourself as a loving person | | | | | |
| Do you feel loved by God? | | | | | |
| Do you enjoy meeting and talking to people? | | | | | |
| Are you satisfied with your present life situation? | | | | | |
| Are you pleased to be you? | | | | | |
| Do you respect yourself? | | | | | |
| Do you take care of your own needs? | | | | | |
| Do you have a balanced life (rest, work, play, etc)? | | | | | |
| Do you enjoy time on your own? | | | | | |
| Do you trust others? | | | | | |
| Do you see yourself as a confident person? | | | | | |
| Do you feel in control of your life? | | | | | |
| Are you considerate of others? | | | | | |
| Do you contribute positively to the lives of others? | | | | | |
| Do you enjoy a relationship with God? | | | | | |

SUB-TOTAL
TOTAL

# THREE

# THE DEVELOPMENT OF OUR
# SELF-CONCEPT

*Teach a child to choose the right path,
and when he is older he will remain upon it.*[1]

Solomon, c. 1000 BC.

There is clearly a big difference between good and poor self-esteem, as has been described earlier. How then do we develop our sense of self? What factors determine our self-concept? Why does one person hate himself and struggle all his life with feelings of inadequacy, while another person can accept herself, get on with living and build good relationships?

All the evidence points to the influence of *the first five years of life*, particularly the relationships children have with the significant adults in their lives. Our self-esteem is not forged for all time by the age of five, but once established it can be hard to change. All conclusions about our world, and how we see ourselves in relationship to it, are built on our earlier experiences and the decisions we made then. But change is possible, with God's help and a desire to be different. Our self-esteem can grow, and it is the purpose of this book to describe ways in which this can take place.

# PRE-BIRTH INFLUENCES

We are born without a developed sense of self. However, pre-natal influences do have a bearing on our later emotional development. Life's experiences do not begin at birth. The child's character and personality are being formed right from conception.

Dr Thomas Verny, a Canadian neurologist and psychologist, has done extensive study on the effect of pre-natal influences on children. In his book, *The Secret Life of the Unborn Child* he states: "A fetus can see, hear, experience, taste and on a primitive level can even learn *in utero*; and most importantly he can feel. A corollary to this discovery is that what a child feels and perceives at this stage begins shaping *his attitudes* and expectations about himself."[2] Dr Verny documents his claims with many examples and references to authentic research.

Research has shown that *unhappy marriages* produced children who as babies were five times more fearful and jumpy than offspring of happy relationships.[3] Also, that a woman locked into a destructive or tension-filled marriage runs more than twice the chance of bearing a psychologically or physically damaged child than a woman in a secure relationship.[4] Dr Frank Lake states: "The origin of many personality disorders and psychosomatic problems can come from experiences during the first trimester [three months] of intra-uterine life."[5]

A study in Germany concluded that the *mother's attitude* had the single greatest effect on how an infant turned out. The second most significant factor affecting the unborn child emotionally was the quality of the woman's relationship with her husband. The children of accepting mothers, who had looked forward to the birth of the child, were much healthier, emotionally and physically at birth and afterwards than children of rejecting mothers.[6]

There is overwhelming evidence that a mother can transfer emotions to her unborn child. Dr Verny explains:

This does not mean that every fleeting worry, doubt or anxiety a woman has rebounds on her child. What matters are deep, persistent patterns of feeling. Chronic anxiety or a wrenching ambivalence about motherhood can leave a deep scar on an unborn child's personality. On the other hand, such life-enhancing emotions as joy, elation and anticipation can contribute significantly to the emotional development of the child.[7]

Dr Luke described the dramatic effect on John the Baptist, who was only at six months intra-uterine development at the time Mary visited his mother. He clearly responded to the joy his mother Elizabeth experienced at the news that Mary brought.[8] It was the habit of Jewish mothers to spend some time in retreat during their pregnancy, preparing themselves emotionally and spiritually for motherhood. Could this have been the purpose of Mary's visit to the godly Elizabeth and Zechariah for three months?[9]

Many psychotherapists and Christian counsellors are convinced that there is much evidence to support the fact that the child in the womb is sensitive to the love of both parents and can be hurt by lack of love.[10] This is not to say that a child's self-esteem is predetermined during intra-uterine development, but the personality is influenced well before birth.

The developing baby responds to what is going on in the outside world.

An example of this comes vividly to mind from our own family. One of our grandsons was born prematurely by caesarian section and was critically ill for the first few days of life. For many weeks before birth our son had talked to him soothingly, telling him of their love and welcome into the world. When the little boy was in the incubator struggling for his life, he would often appear restless and agitated. At these times, Geoff would talk to him calmly, assuring him that everything was all right. The effect was immediate, and as he recognised his father's voice he would become quieter.

# CHILDHOOD

After birth, we are constantly exposed to influences in our lives from our parents and family as well as from many other sources. Some of these build us up in our sense of identity and self-worth, while others have the opposite effect. Negative messages affect most people more easily and more deeply than positive ones. This is especially true for people who already have developed low self-esteem. They readily absorb further negative messages, which confirm their negative view of themselves. Conversely, they will often block or deny any positive influences. The longer this involuted thinking continues, the harder it is to challenge and change. During these early years, we all ask two basic questions about life:

1) **Who am I?** This is the first thing we want to know. The conclusions we come to are based to a

large extent on what is reflected back to us by others. We are very sensitive to how they see us and what they say about us, and it is not until we are older that we have the capacity to evaluate ourselves more objectively. For young children, significant adults like parents, older siblings and teachers, become *the mirrors in which they see themselves*. For teenagers, their peer group is usually more important in this regard.

Unlike good quality glass mirrors, people mirrors can reflect back different pictures of ourselves, each depending more on what the mirror is like than on what we are like. Mirrors can be cracked! Some "mirrors" will give us a positive image and others a negative one. Also, the mental image of ourselves that follows other people's reactions can be distorted, especially when we are young. It is rather like looking in a comic mirror in a fun park, and seeing myself too tall or too fat. What I think I see reflected back from you may be an inaccurate picture of myself. For example, when a child reaches out for affection from a parent and does not get it, he may interpret this as: "Mummy doesn't love me"; when the truth is mother is preoccupied or perhaps struggling with her own pain at that time.

The Bible provides us with an accurate mirror of ourselves, not only of our sin and imperfection, but also of our inherent beauty – being made in the image of God – and of our importance to him. But when some people read the Bible they fail to absorb the many positive messages from God about their value and worth to him. Instead, their negative view of themselves is reinforced by a distorted theology.

2) **What is my world like?** This is probably the next important question that children ask. The answers depend on their experiences of life,

and particularly on the quality of the parent–child relationships. By about the age of two, a child has developed an attitude of *basic trust* (or mistrust). Erik Erikson first coined this term to describe "whether the world is a good and satisfying place to live or a source of pain, misery, frustration and uncertainty."[11] He claimed that the absence of basic trust is associated with the development of schizophrenia and depression in later life.

Unless children learn to trust their early caregivers, their world becomes very insecure. "Without basic trust, a child cannot establish autonomy; the trust in himself that enables him, by successive stages, to separate his identity from his parents . . . and stand on his own two feet as an integrated individual."[12] Basic trust is one of a number of factors which is necessary for the development of self-esteem. The most important one is the *consistent experience of love*. But the supply of love in a child's life can be cut off in many ways.

## Interrupted love process

The flow of love from parents to children can be interrupted for a variety of reasons. One parent may have died when the child was young. Circumstances may make it necessary for one or both parents to be absent for a significant period of time. For example, the nature of their work may require a period of absence from the family for a business trip; either the child or a parent may experience a prolonged illness, necessitating hospitalisation. These separations can be very traumatic, particularly for children between the ages of six months and three years.

Other events such as war or natural disasters may greatly disturb family life. This does not mean that parents love their children any less, but often this is how the child interprets the situation. *Marriage break-up* will undoubtedly have profound effects on children. Children may even blame themselves for what has happened, e.g. "If I hadn't been naughty, Daddy wouldn't have left."

It is quite common for one of the parents (usually the father) to be *emotionally absent*, even though physically present in the family. He may be a very "remote" person, unable to express his feelings and preoccupied with his work. As a result, the children do not feel loved by him, even though deep down he may love them very much.

Often it is only in the mind of the child that these situations are a problem. If children knew how to express these thoughts and feelings, their misconceptions might be corrected. Children may experience a number of the negative influences listed in this chapter, not so much by design as by default. But these can still have a significant effect on their self-esteem. If the child already has started to develop low self-esteem, the effect will be even greater.

## Fear of abandonment

All children are terrified by the possibility of being abandoned. This fear of abandonment starts at about the age of six months, at the time when the young child is beginning to realise that she is a separate identity from her primary care-giver and provider, usually her mother. To a child, being abandoned by parents is a fate as bad as death.[13]

Abandonment can happen physically, as described in the previous section. But it can also be experienced psychologically by children whose parents are unable or unwilling to invest time and emotional energy in them. These children grow up feeling that they are of little worth, likely to be rejected by others and have a poor sense of basic trust. This sets the stage for the development of low self-esteem. Most children who have been adopted struggle at some stage with feelings of being rejected or abandoned by their birth parents.

We will now discuss some of the positive and negative factors that influence the development of a proper sense of self-worth as we grow up.

# POSITIVE INFLUENCES

## Unconditional love

This is *the key*. It is the soil in which good self-esteem grows. Unconditional love means loving people irrespective of how they look or act. It means accepting them for who they are, not for what they do. It means valuing them for their intrinsic worth, not on the basis of their abilities or liabilities. It means loving them even if they do not, or are unable to love you in return. C.S. Lewis defined this kind of love as "gift-love" as opposed to "need-love" in his classic book *The Four Loves*.[14] It is the kind of love the New Testament writers refer to when they use the word "agape". Agape-love is more related to the will than to the emotions. It is a commitment to love even the unlovable or unresponsive person unconditionally.

If we love our children conditionally, only when they please us or fulfil our expectations of them, they will not feel genuinely loved. They will feel constantly guilty that they have not done enough to earn our love. "This in turn makes them feel insecure, damages their self image, and actually prevents them from developing more mature behaviour."[15] John Powell expresses it this way: "Unconditional love is liberating. It frees the loved one to be authentic and real. Conditional love leaves the loved one only the course of conformity."[16]

Unconditional love is not just difficult, it is impossible in our own strength! As a parent, as a lover, or as a friend I am aware that I need God's input into my life to give me the strength to love unconditionally. Unconditional love is essentially a divine form of loving. This is how God loves. God's love is not dependent on our loving him first, or even in return. He loves us just as much whether we love him or turn our backs on him.

To be nurtured in such love is the birthright of all children. A child who has experienced unconditional love, even imperfectly from an imperfect parent, will have the foundation on which to build his or her sense of self-worth. Erich Fromm states in his book *The Art of Loving*:

All experiences become crystallized and integrated in the experience: I am loved. I am loved because I am my mother's child. I am loved because I am helpless. I am loved because I am beautiful, admirable. I am loved because mother needs me. To put it in a more general formula: I am loved for what I am, or perhaps more accurately: I am loved because I am.[17]

We not only need to experience this kind of loving as infants, but throughout our early years, if we are to be able to love ourselves and others adequately. Few people have known that kind of loving constantly as they grew up, even in the most loving of homes. Even the very best parents are fallible. Many have limited parenting skills, and do not really know how to express their love.

In what ways is unconditional love communicated?

*Focused attention*

A good way to describe the process of giving a child unconditional love is to think of giving him or her our focused attention. It is not possible to do this all the time, nor would it be desirable. But this is how people discover they are really loved.

Focused attention means giving myself totally to another person at that time. It means being completely "present" for that person. This is probably *our most basic human need*: to be noticed and to be significant to at least one other person. Children who experience this in the early years of life develop a sense of worth and value. As they grow older, they learn to fit into a society where other people also have this need, which they can try to meet. But if a person has never experienced being significant to someone else, it is very hard, if not impossible to reach out to another human being in true love. This need for focused attention is as true for teenagers, as for young children. "Parents need to know how to genuinely and effectually *transmit* their love to their teenager."[18]

There are several ways in which focused attention can be expressed:

**Time**. Focused attention is communicated first and foremost to children by *giving them our time*. Many parents will give money or material possessions to their children far sooner than they will give their time. They may make great sacrifices to ensure their children have a good education or financial security, but may not spend five minutes a day of quality time with each of them. Children are often bad spellers and usually spell love: T I M E. Good families take time but bad families take more time!

Adults often want the time they spend with children to be productive, doing something "useful" or talking about something "worthwhile". The most important reason for spending time with a child is *to be together*. This communicates the message "I care about you"; "You are important to me"; "You are significant". Children will only talk about important things to people who have time for them, time to listen.

I (John) will never forget when one of my daughters said to me some years ago: "Dad, have you got your diary handy?" When I produced it she said, "Please may I make a booking for an appointment?" I realised that my diary was often full of appointments for other people rather than for those dearest to me. I made some radical changes in my life that day in response to that gentle hint!

Focused attention becomes reality to children in the way we use our *ears*, our *eyes* and our *hands*.

**Listening.** Children feel significant when they are listened to. The old adage: "Children should be seen and not heard", is not true. Children should be *seen and heard*. They also have to learn to be silent and listen to others appropriately. But children who are not listened to or taken seriously grow up believing they are of no value. Home should be a place where children can think out loud safely, where they can talk and be taken seriously. Listening with focused attention is hard work. I must set aside my own agenda for the time being in order to focus on yours. Listening builds a child's self – esteem. It communicates the message: "What you say is important to me, therefore *you are important to me*", even if what is said doesn't make too much sense to either of us!

**Eye contact**. Eye contact is a way of loving and a way of touching.[19] The poet Yeats expressed it: "Love comes in at the eyes." The eye is the window of the soul. Jesus spoke of the significance of the eyes: "The eye is the lamp of the body."[20] Caring eye contact communicates the message: "I see you, and I like what I see." It also communicates *respect*. In fact, the word "respect" is derived from the Latin word "respicere" which means "to look at". To look you in the eye says: "I respect your unique individuality. You are a person of worth." We acknowledge that there is some variation in the use of eye contact from culture to culture.[21]

Little children especially need lots of eye contact, but unless adults bend down to talk with them, they often miss out. This is one of the reasons young children like to climb on your knee, because in this position your eyes are at the same level as theirs. Some children only receive eye contact from their parents when they have done something wrong! Teenagers also need a lot of positive eye contact, even in times of conflict. This can say: "I may not approve of what you are doing, but I approve of you."

**Touch**. We are all born with about 640,000 touch detectors in our skin, which need stimulation.[22] We all have a "skin hunger".[23]

Researchers have demonstrated that touch is the first of the senses to develop early in intra-uterine life,[24] and probably the last to go when we are dying.

Healthy touch is a powerful way to communicate the message "I love you . . . you're OK". *Touching is loving.* It nourishes and brings healing. It brings a sense of self-worth. A child who is not touched concludes deep down in his subconscious, "I'm not worth touching". Sadly, some children have also been touched inappropriately and physically or sexually abused. Unhealthy touch is very damaging.

But many studies have proved the importance of touch for young children and indeed for all animals.[25] Children who are deprived of touch fail to thrive physically and deteriorate mentally. This is called *Maternal Deprivation Syndrome*, and one of the main factors causing this condition, and its high mortality, is lack of touch. Bertrand Russell pointed out that it is touch which gives us a sense of reality. Jules Older, in his superb book *Touching is Healing* summarises it this way:

> The hugged child will thrive.
> The hit child will survive.
> The untouched child will die.[26]

**Praise**. A child needs praise and lots of it! For some reason, the Victorian belief still lingers in the minds of many parents that too much praise is bad for children and will give them "swelled heads". Providing it is genuine and not given in order to manipulate, there is no limit to the amount of affirmation and praise a child can have. "We parents are much more in danger of perpetuating our children's fear of failure than of making them unjustly proud."[27]

Here is a summary of the positive influences that build self-esteem:

## THE FOUR A's

ATTENTION       They look at me and I know
                I'm loved and respected. They
                spend time with me which
                means they are interested in
                me. They listen to me and
                I feel heard. They touch me
                and I feel good about myself.
ACCEPTANCE      I am valued for who I am, not
                on the basis of what I do or
                do not do. So I know I am
                a worthwhile member of my
                family and community.
AFFIRMATION     I am praised for who I am
                as well as what I do, so I
                feel confident that I am both
                lovable and capable.
AFFECTION       I am loved unconditionally
                and know I am special.

But not all the experiences of our early childhood are
positive. We live in an imperfect world and parents
are not perfect, though they usually do the best they
can for their children.


# NEGATIVE INFLUENCES

The things that inhibit the development of a good
self-esteem are essentially the absence of the above
positive factors; in particular, not experiencing unconditional love.

## Conditional love

All love that is offered on the basis of conditions set
by the lover is conditional love, however reasonable
the conditions. Most of the loving that people experience as they grow up is conditional:

- Mummy will love you, "IF you play nicely;
  IF you don't make too much noise; IF you
  keep your room tidy; IF . . ."
- Parents will love you, IF you do well at school;
  IF you are good at sport; IF you accept their
  values; IF you marry the right person . . .
- The world loves you, IF you are good looking, intelligent, make a lot of money, drive
  a flash car, live in the right suburb . . .

In the world most of us grew up in, love and respect
had to be earned or deserved. We have been told by
many people that as children they tried very hard to
please their parents, but "never quite made it". They
were not able to satisfy their parents' expectations.
They were "never quite good enough". Consequently,
like Julie in the last chapter, they did not feel they
deserved to be loved.

Erich Fromm writes forcefully on this:

Unconditional love corresponds to one of the
deepest longings, not only of the child, but
of every human being; on the other hand to
be loved because of one's merit, because one
deserves it, always leaves doubt – maybe I did
not please the person whom I want to love me,
maybe this, maybe that – there is always the
fear that love could disappear. Furthermore,

'deserved' love easily leaves a bitter feeling that one is not loved for oneself, that one is loved only because one pleases, in the last analysis, that one is not loved but used.[28]

## Lack of focused attention

When focused attention is missing during early development, a child questions whether he is important to anyone. She may grow up in a home with loving parents, but still feel she has missed out. This is particularly true of the compliant child, who is never any trouble and always tries to please. So often, this behaviour is taken for granted by parents, who are very busy with the tasks of caring and providing. The unco-operative child in a family often gets more attention than the "good" ones. Bad behaviour is frequently an attempt to obtain some attention. Even a smack is preferable to no touch or being ignored!

The problem with parenting is that there are no "dummy runs", and we don't know much about it until the job is over. For example, we believed that our five children, who are fairly close together in age, should all have the same treatment, with no favouritism. We spent many hours doing things together as a family, reading books together and enjoying family fun. These were great times. But if we had our chance over again, we would both try to have a special time with each child regularly, as well as family togetherness. Susanna Wesley spent one hour a week with each of her seventeen children. No wonder there was a John and a Charles Wesley in our church heritage.

Nigel's story illustrates the connection between his experience as a child and his relationships as an adult. He grew up in a missionary family and his parents were deeply committed to their work. Nigel and his wife came to us because they found it difficult to experience the emotional intimacy and closeness they had hoped for in their marriage. Although a committed Christian and a leader in his church, Nigel felt a hypocrite. "When I pray," he said, "it's like my prayers don't reach higher than the ceiling. God seems so far away." We invited him to tell us some memories of his childhood.

I remember my father as a very hard-working and devoted missionary. He spent a lot of time in his office, at the end of a long corridor. Sometimes I wanted to be with him and would knock on his door. Often he sent me away, but occasionally he would invite me to sit on a chair and tell him what I had been doing or how I was getting on with my school lessons, which I did by correspondence at home. He never came out to play games with me.

With tears in his eyes he told us:

When I was older I was sent away to boarding school and contact with my parents was by weekly letter. I always remember, the first page of their reply was a detailed list of the spelling mistakes in my last letter. Later I went to College. After two years I wrote home excitedly to say I was halfway through my course. They replied to the effect that I shouldn't be too excited yet as I still had another two years of hard work. I know they wanted the best for me, but I don't ever remember my parents praising me. They had very high expectations of us children, and it seemed I could never please them.

It was easy to understand why Nigel found it difficult to be close to anyone, even his wife; and why God seemed such a remote figure, out of reach. It was a lot harder for him to deal with those memories and discover his worth and value.

One helpful way of healing painful memories of the past is to invite Jesus into the situation. After all, time is a human invention. With God it is the eternal present. As a person relives the painful memory, Jesus is invited to be present in all his love and healing power to minister to the hurting child. As God's love and presence is experienced in this way, so the painful trauma is soothed and healed. This "healing of the memories", of course, is only the start. But it is a powerful way of clearing blocks to growth. Old patterns and thinking still have to be replaced by new ones in order to move on to spiritual and psychological wholeness and maturity in Christ.

## Lack of praise

Traditionally in the Western world the idea has been taught that children should not be praised, because of the danger of making them proud or boastful. There is absolutely no justification for this and in fact the reverse is true. A child who has not been appropriately affirmed and praised often grows up with an excessive need for attention and praise and may go to great lengths to try to obtain it. This has been called "*Deprivation Neurosis Syndrome*".[29] A person with this syndrome is likely to be self-centred. He is uncertain of his real abilities and qualities and is always trying to prove himself. Consequently, he may become socially isolated and overly dependent on others. He or she will almost certainly suffer from low self-esteem.

Children tend to value themselves *to the extent they have been valued*. This is a very important principle. "The feeling of being valuable – I am a valuable person – is essential to mental health and is a cornerstone of self-discipline."[30]

Margaret is a very competent and capable person, who spent some years as a missionary. But she had a very low self-esteem and saw herself of little value. We asked her how much praise she got as a child. She could only recollect one occasion, when her mother complimented her on completing her university degree. Her father overheard and actually stopped his wife in mid sentence, "In case Margaret should become too proud," he said.

In seminars on self-esteem, we have frequently asked, "How many of you have been praised or complimented this week at work for something you have done?" It is usually about 5 per cent of the audience. People who have seldom been praised naturally find it difficult to praise others and so the cycle continues.

## Negative "parent" messages

As we grow up we receive many messages about ourselves. Some are positive but most are negative. Here are a few typical negative messages, from "parents", i.e. the significant adults in our lives:

"You'll never make it!"
"When are you going to grow up?"
"You always mess things up."
"You're just like your mother."
"You'd better not try."
"After all we've done for you!"
"How dumb can you be?"
"Here, let me do that for you."
"Hurry up!"
"Late, again."
"You wouldn't understand."
"You're always so clumsy."

These messages are never lost, but they can be challenged and changed. We all need to "be made new in the attitude of your minds".[31] It may take about 100 positive messages subsequently to undo one negative one that a child has believed and internalised. This is because we so readily turn negative messages we have received into a permanent mind set.

## SUMMARY

In this chapter we have briefly reviewed positive and negative influences that affect the development of our self-image and identity. Our intention is not to apportion blame, rather to increase awareness and understanding. God has created us with the ability to make choices, and it is *choice* not *chance* which determines who we become. Two children brought up in the same home, who receive essentially the same treatment, may have very different levels of self-esteem. It is not unusual to meet people who have had a very disadvantaged childhood but who feel good about themselves and about life. *Mister*

*God This Is Anna* is a moving story of a little girl who was abandoned in the East End of London, and who was able to put the past behind her and develop a wonderful self-image.[32]

We take responsibility for our self-esteem by the choices we make. No one can *give* us good or bad self-esteem, even though our experiences with the significant people in our lives have a powerful influence on us. Someone has put it this way:

> Who we are is God's gift to us,
> Who we become is our gift to God.

# REFLECTIONS AND EXERCISES

1 Write down what you know about the circumstances of your conception and nine months in
the womb. Do you know what was happening
for your mother and the family at that time?
Was your mother happy/relaxed/stressed out/fear-
ful, etc., while she was carrying you? (This may
require some help from parents, or other family
members.)

- Were you a wanted child, by both your father
  and mother? Were you welcomed into the
  family with great excitement? Was your birth
  easy or difficult? Take note of your hunches
  and feelings about the above, even if you are
  unable to verify them.
- Spend some time in prayer:
  - Thank God for your parents who gave you
    life, especially for your mother who gave
    you birth.
  - Ask the Holy Spirit to reveal to you any-
    thing that you should know about your life
    before birth.
  - Ask the Lord to heal you of any trauma
    that you may have experienced during
    those hidden months, for whatever reason.
- If your parents are still alive, thank them for
  bringing you into the world and tell them that
  you love them.

2 Choose a quite place where you will not be disturbed. Relax for a while, and then meditate on
Psalm 139:13–16.

- Write down in your journal any thoughts or
  insights that come to you.

3 What memories do you have of positive influences in your childhood years such as: quality time spent with parents or other people important to you; really being listened to; being affirmed and encouraged in what you were interested in or wanted to do; being told that you were loved, etc?

- Record these in your journal and think about them. Thank God for them.
- If you are in a group situation, share them with others.

4 How much touch did you receive as a child? Do you think this was adequate? Do you think there is any relationship between the amount of healthy touch you received then and your comfort/discomfort with touch now?

- How much touch do you get in your life at present? Do you wish you had more, and if so, how could this be achieved? We have no right to invade other people's space, but we can invite them to invade ours!
- If you are in a group, discuss ways in which you could do this, e.g. offering one another a hug, a shoulder massage, a back rub or a foot massage at the start or end of the session.
- How could you increase the amount of appropriate touch experienced in your family or church fellowship? There are probably many touch-deprived people in every church. What could you do to help them receive more touch?

5 How much conditional love did you receive as a child, i.e. "You will be loved IF . . .?" Can you think of times you experienced genuine unconditional love? How would you describe the difference?

- Share some of these incidents in the group or
  in pairs.
- Compare the love you have experienced with
  1 Corinthians 13:4–7.

6 Reflect on your early childhood years. Did you
  experience any interruption in the "love process"?
  Examples of this would be: a prolonged period of
  hospitalisation; going to boarding school; absence
  of your parents due to sickness, or any other
  reason. Perhaps you had an "emotionally absent"
  parent.

- In what ways do you think this had an impact
  on you, especially your sense of self-worth?
  (It may or may not have affected you significantly, depending on your choices at the
  time.)

7 Think about the relationship you had with your
  father. If for some reason, such as death or marriage break-up you cannot remember your father,
  think of a relationship you had with another
  significant male figure, such as grandfather or
  uncle.

- Ask yourself these questions:
  - Did he spend time with me; play with me;
    hug me; tell me he loved me; affirm me
    as a person; make me feel good about
    my gender; teach me; discipline me; pray
    with me?
  - What do you think his feelings were for
    you? Did he love you, accept you, feel proud
    of you?
  - What were your feelings about him? Did

you love him; fear him; feel safe with him;
respect him?
- Do the same exercise, thinking about your
mother this time.
- Reflect on this experience, and then:
  - Thank God for all the good memories you
    have.
  - Grieve for the things you missed out on.
    Identify the losses. Tell God about them.
    Shed a few tears if you need to.
  - If you can honestly do so, forgive your
    parents for their short-comings, and then
    let go of the hurts.
  - Ask God to "re-parent" you in these mis-
    sing areas. Read 2 Corinthians 6:18. Claim
    this as a promise for yourself.

8 As we grow up we often receive confusing answers
to the basic question: "Who am I?" It is helpful
to clarify this again and again as an adult, with
more mature insights, and because we are always
changing.

- If you are on your own, write down as many
  answers as you can to this question. For example: "I am a woman/man, a wife/husband, a
  mother/father, a teacher, a caring person, a
  child of God, insecure some times, a visionary,
  a positive person, a growing person . . ."
- If you are in a group situation, form pairs
  and one of you ask the other: "Who are you?"
  Keep asking this question until your partner
  runs out of answers. Then change over and
  repeat the process. Help each other explore
  the answers. Affirm one another for what is
  shared.

- This is a very good exercise for couples to do together. This is similar to exercise 2 at the end of Chapter 1. There is value in repeating the exercise, especially with a different person.

9  If you are in a group, form pairs. Spend at least two minutes quietly looking into each other's eyes, without speaking. At the same time, mentally reflect on how much you appreciate and value the other person. (Some soft background music could be helpful.)

- Discuss together how you experienced this exercise.
- Share your conclusions in the larger group.

10  Lord Alfred Tennyson wrote: "I am part of all I have met." This is true for all of us. List in your journal people you have met who have influenced you significantly, either positively or negatively, in the development of your sense of self-worth.

# FOUR

# CONSEQUENCES OF LOW SELF-ESTEEM

*Whoever has will be given more, and he will have an abundance.*
*Whoever does not have, even what he has will be taken from him.*[1]

Jesus

Low self-esteem affects what we feel about ourselves and how we relate to others. The two cannot be separated. If each of us lived on our own desert island, a low self image would not be such a problem. But as John Donne put it so graphically: "No man is an island, entire of itself; every man is a piece of the Continent, part of the main."[2]

The fact is, we were not created to live on our own: "The Lord God said, "It is not good for the man to be alone. I will make a helper suitable for him."[3] Note that the word "man" in this statement is not the Hebrew word *"ish"*, meaning man, male; but *"adam"*, the generic word for mankind, male and female. God is not merely stating that Adam needed a wife; rather, that human beings are not designed to exist in isolation. We have been created for relationship. This is a consequence of being created in the image of a triune God, who lives in relationship: "Let **us** make man in **our** image"[4] (our emphasis). So, if relationships are part of being human, and our self-esteem affects our relationships so much, it is important that we have a good self-concept.

When people have low self-esteem, how do they relate: to themselves, to others and to God? In this chapter, we will identify some common behaviours displayed by people who have a low self-esteem. Then we will explore how low self-esteem affects relationships.

# COMPENSATING BEHAVIOURS FOR LOW SELF-ESTEEM

The behaviour of people reflects how they feel about themselves. If they do not feel good about themselves it stands out like the proverbial sore thumb. The following are some of the ways in which people try to deal with the pain inside, the pain of feeling inadequate or not quite good enough. You may recognise some of these in yourself, as you read on, because we all use them at times. Unfortunately, they do nothing to relieve the pain, nor do they help relationships.

## Excessive shyness

People often use shyness in an attempt to insulate themselves against failure and rejection. Thus, someone becomes a loner or a very "remote" person, who will not relate to others. In social settings, it is safer to be a "wallflower". Try to become invisible, because if you are noticed, people might discover what you are really like. So, don't take any risks. In a group situation one's internal dialogue may go something like this: "Whatever can I say to these clever people, they seem to be so much more knowledgeable than I am. I don't want to look dumb, so I'd better keep quiet."

## Putting yourself down

People use this ploy for a variety of reasons. If you put yourself down first, this may avoid the pain of someone else doing so! Also, it could just be that if you put yourself down, someone may deny it, which might make you feel better. On the other hand, people with low self-esteem often will not accept an affirmation and usually dismiss compliments. People who consistently put themselves down are likely to criticise others.

Marion was a capable person. She was a good cook and dressmaker, making all her own clothes. If anyone complimented her about a cake she had made, Marion would say, "It is not as nice as the last one". The clothes she made were beautifully finished. She was pleased if someone remarked on a new dress, but invariably pointed out a minor fault. In effect, she was not saying: "The dress is no good," but "I'm not much good".

## Drawing attention to yourself

This is another evidence of insecurity. Attention seeking is often apparent in young children when they are in an unfamiliar environment or when their parents are focusing their attention on others. This behaviour seems to be the opposite of shyness but still reflects a poor self-esteem. It shows up often in a group situation, where one person has to be the centre of attention. He will try to steal the limelight or become "the life and soul of the party" by monopolising the conversation or telling all the jokes. This is characteristic behaviour of a person who missed out on focused attention as a child.

## Boasting

Boasting, bragging or exaggerating are classic ploys of people who feel unsure of themselves and are trying to bolster their sagging self-image or present themselves looking larger than life. Some people with a poor self-concept will take every opportunity to talk about their achievements or what they own. They see their achievements and possessions as extensions of themselves which will gain the attention that they so desperately need.

## Being dogmatic

People with low self-esteem find it shattering to their fragile egos to be proved wrong. So they always have to appear to win an argument and may stubbornly refuse to admit defeat, even when it is so obvious to everyone else! This is different from having thought-out convictions and holding one's ground about them, which is evidence of healthy self-esteem. Dogmatic thinking is the inability to see another person's point of view, or the refusal to admit that I may be wrong. For people with a poor self-image, to be wrong in one's thinking is to be wrong as a person. They are unable to differentiate between the two. Consequently, they will usually find it difficult, if not impossible, to apologise.

## Suspicion and criticism

The ability to evaluate objectively the world around us is a sign of maturity. But to be excessively critical, suspicious and to trust nobody, is evidence of insecurity. People with a poor self-concept often become cynical and highly critical of others. They put others down and are unable to see good in people. Obviously, people who put themselves down will be likely to do this to others. This tends to alienate them from other people, which may be their subconscious goal anyway because being close to others is risky.

## Rigid thinking

People who are insecure often become rigid, "black-and-white" thinkers. (See page 24.) They may have fads about diet or routines. Legalistic religious thinking is another example of this. Paul describes such a person as "the weaker brother".[5] It is much safer for them to live by rigid rules and regulations than to live by grace. Some people without a faith can be even more rigid in their thinking, constantly pointing out reasons why there cannot be a God. This is because if they are wrong, they not only have to revise their opinions but also their view of themselves.

## Aggression

Aggressive behaviour is sometimes seen as strength. In fact, it is *evidence of weakness*. To force my will on you is a sign of my own insecurity. A man who does not know how to cope with an equal relationship in marriage may try to resolve the dilemma by dominating his wife and children or even becoming violent. Insecure people, with a low self-esteem, often want to control others.

There are essentially three ways in which people behave in their relationships: being *passive, assertive* or *aggressive*. Some people, who are aware of their passive behaviour, attend assertiveness courses and end up aggressive! Both passive and aggressive behaviours demonstrate low self-esteem. Appropriate assertiveness is a reflection of good self-esteem. (See Chapter 9 for further comments on assertiveness.)

*Workaholism*

A compulsive urge to be always doing something may reflect insecurity and a feeling of inadequacy. This can have many causes. It may be that a parent or a colleague is a workaholic, and I feel guilty if I don't try to keep up. Perhaps I have received the "parent message" described in the last chapter: "You'll never make it". So I spend my life trying to change that. In my mind I never do "make it", and this becomes the "slave-driver", urging me on to work compulsively.

Workaholism has been described as a *special addiction of the religious person* which can become a "false religion".[6] This is a consequence of the so-called "Protestant work ethic" or such teaching as: "To work is to pray". There is nothing wrong with this attitude in its proper place. Work is God ordained.[7] But anything can become a false god in our lives.

Norman came for counselling because of symptoms of stress. He was in a state of "burnout", not coping with his job. He was a very good accountant, but worked excessively long hours. This was causing marital disharmony. Norman grew up in a home where his father was a very successful business executive and worked about twelve hours in his office most days. He had no memory of his father spending time with him, playing or doing things together. "Dad never once came to watch a sports event where I was competing, and I was a champion runner at school." His father took an interest in Norman's school reports, and was quick to notice if he got a "B" or a "C" for any subject, but never complimented him for getting an "A". "I suppose he just expected that all my marks would be A's," said Norman, "but I always felt that whatever I did was never quite good enough for Dad. It seemed that I could never please him."

Norman was a lay preacher and felt devalued if people did not compliment him after he had preached a sermon. He was devastated by any negative comments. Helping him deal with his stress involved looking at self-esteem issues. Eventually he came to see that his worth did not depend on his ability to achieve, but on who he was. He recovered from burnout and his life returned to a more even keel. Although he still worked hard, Norman built some *balance* into his life, and relationships at home improved.

Another cause of excessive work behaviour is *trying to please everyone*. This, of course, is impossible, but a lot of people try hard to do it. Many women pick up this message in our society: "You must please everyone, especially men." This can become an intolerable burden. Bill Cosby said: "I don't know the key to success, but the key to failure is to try to please everybody!"

Wanting to please everyone was a decision I (John) made early in life. "No" was the very first word I ever learned, but my mother convinced me by the age of three that it was a naughty word! So I stopped saying "No". I was about forty before I learned to say "No" comfortably as well as firmly. My problem was this: if I said "No" to you, you might not like me and I could not cope with that. So I tended to take on more

requests for work than was reasonable and became
over-loaded. I have met many other people with this
problem.

Learning to say "No" implies that I have a right
to say "No". So the first step involves dealing with
the issue of my self-worth. If I am a person of worth,
I have the right to decide how I should spend my
time. I do not have to try to please everybody. This
does not mean I should go to the other extreme and
become inconsiderate of others. But if I cannot say
"No", it means that I cannot really say "Yes" either.
"Yes" has become just a knee-jerk reflex rather than
a conscious decision. St Paul made some pertinent
comments on this issue: "I am not trying to please
you by sweet talk and flattery; no, I am trying to
please God. If I were still trying to please men I
could not be Christ's servant" and "Our aim is to
please him always in everything we do."[8]

\* \* \*

We have listed some common compensating behaviours used by people who have low self-esteem.
Freud, in 1894, described them as "ego defences".[9]
Psychologists and psychiatrists today call them
*defence mechanisms*: "The ways people react to
frustration and conflict by deceiving themselves
about their real desires and goals in order to maintain their self-esteem and avoid anxiety."[10] We use
defences to hide our weaknesses not our strengths.
Christians are just as prone to subconscious defence
mechanisms as anyone else. However, they now have
available to them healthy, biblical ways of dealing
with emotional pain.[11]

As children, we instinctively resort to these ways
of defending our egos. But they are inappropriate

ways of coping with life as adults. They become "masks" behind which we hide our real selves. John Powell calls this a *distorted vision of ourselves*,[12] which warps the way we react in our world, and prevents us from being "fully alive".

Dr Garry Collins describes *The Vicious Circle of Inferiority*. He says:

> The problem with convincing others we are inferior is that before long we end up convincing ourselves ... And if we succeed in convincing ourselves that we are inferior in order to be consistent with our convictions, we act in an inferior way. Notice in Figure 2 that once we put in an inferior performance, this comes back as proof to ourselves and to others that we are indeed inferior. This is called a vicious circle.

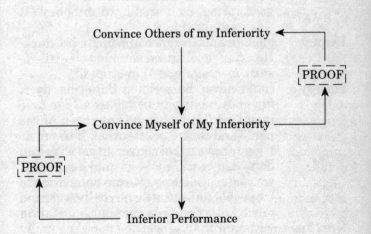

**Figure 2.** The Inferiority Cycle

A person can get onto the cycle at any point, and when he moves in the direction of the arrows, his feelings of inferiority increase and his performance gets worse.[13]

# SNOW WHITE AND THE SEVEN DWARFS

This fairy story[14] is a subtle parable of some of the ways in which people try to compensate for a low self-image. The dwarfs were little people, at least that is how they thought of themselves. They all wore what we have called "labels", "masks" or "T-shirt messages". Do you remember them?

**Grumpy**   was the pessimist, with a negative view of everything. He went around with a chip on his shoulder. He did not feel very good inside, so it was hard to believe it was good outside.

**Dopey**   gave the appearance of being a bit thick. He often apologised for himself. His T-shirt message was "I'm stupid!".

**Happy**   could never be serious. Being happy is fine, but having to be *happy all the time* is unreal. He had to be the clown of the party and centre of attention. If someone tried to have a real conversation with him he would crack a joke or make a pun. It was safer that way. It was dangerous to let people find out who he really was, and much better to keep them at a distance.

**Bashful**   withdrew from people and hoped he would not be noticed. His motto was: "Never speak unless you are spoken to because you may give away the fact that you are an inferior person."

**Sleepy** was always a bit slow and often missed out on what went on in the group. He was often late for appointments. When he felt nervous he would yawn and was tired most of the time.

**Sneezy** had frequent psychosomatic illnesses and always seemed to suffer from a cold or allergy. Often a headache would prevent him from joining in with the others. His T-shirt message said: "I'm not very strong. Please look after me."

**Doc** was the "Smart Alec" of the bunch, the "wise-guy", with an explanation for everything. He had to contradict other people's opinions and was dogmatic, cynical and hypercritical.

What we have just described were their defence mechanisms that had *become their mind-set*. Their vision of themselves was distorted. It is not certain who gave them their names in the Walt Disney version of the story, but the person must have been a shrewd observer of human nature, because many people react like the dwarfs when they do not feel good about themselves. You will meet some of these "dwarfs" in real life.

What about Snow White? What did she do for them? At first appearances all she did was to love them, and they certainly needed that. However, it could be that she also "smothered" them. She was a "rescuer". She did their washing, mending, ironing and cooking. She put them to bed and coddled them when they were sick. Probably, she reinforced their pathology! It was not an angel they needed to live with them, but another dwarf *who did not think like a dwarf*.

They needed someone who could demonstrate that they could live without their labels; that there is a healthier way to live than to hide behind a mask. We too need to be shown how to live, and someone actually came 2000 years ago for this purpose: "Christ took our human nature and lived here on earth among us and was full of loving forgiveness and truth. And some of us have seen his glory – the glory of the only Son of the heavenly Father."[15]

\* \* \*

Low self-esteem not only causes minor behaviourisms, such as have been described above, but can affect us very deeply in our personalities and relationships.

# PERSONAL CONSEQUENCES OF LOW SELF-ESTEEM

*Depression*

There are a number of causes of depression. Here is a simple but useful summary.

i) Depression can be *secondary* to an illness like influenza, or a side effect of some medications.
ii) It can be *Reactive* Depression, following a loss or bereavement.
iii) Depression can be a *disease* in itself, such as when the body is suffering from a biochemical disorder in the brain.

But whatever the cause of depression, low self-esteem will *aggravate the problem*. To belittle myself constantly, to reject myself and believe that I am a failure, prepares the ground thoroughly for a depressive illness to set in and it will certainly delay recovery, whatever the cause of the depression.

This process has been well described by Aaron Beck[16] as a *Cognitive Triad* which characterises depression. A depressed person:

1) *Sees himself or herself negatively*: "I am incompetent, stupid and worthless. Life's unpleasant experiences and problems are my fault because I lack the qualities necessary for a happy and contented life."
2) *Sees life negatively*: "The world makes too many demands. Life is unfair and nobody loves me. Other people don't have these problems."
3) *Sees the future negatively*: "Nothing will ever change. I'm sure to fail in anything I do. There is no hope."

Depression and low self-esteem are clearly linked. Ego psychologists say that depression is often precipitated by a conflict between one's actual ego state (who I am), and one's ideal ego state (who I would like to be). This results in lowered self-esteem.[17] Dr James Dobson has studied the problem of depression in women. His research indicated that 50 per cent of women ranked low self-esteem as the *chief cause* of depression for them, and 80 per cent placed it in the top five.[18]

## Stress

Coping with low self-esteem adds a constant strain and tension to a person's life. It uses up so much psychic energy to always be on guard, defensive, fearful that someone might show you up to be the inadequate person you think you are. People with a poor self-concept carry around an ache inside they cannot ignore. This is stressful in itself, and makes it so much harder to cope with the stressors in the environment and the pressures of every day living.

## Guilt

People often feel very guilty when they think of themselves as failures and misfits. Paul Tournier claimed that: "All inferiority is experienced as guilt."[19] Their constant preoccupation is: "I should do better", or "I have failed, again". This is false guilt, which is a very different thing from real guilt, although it feels the same. These kinds of guilt feelings are aggravated in a depressive illness.

Tournier defines *false guilt*, which he also calls "functional guilt", as follows:

> A feeling of "functional guilt" is one which results from social suggestion, fear of taboos or of losing the love of others ... A feeling of "value guilt" is the genuine consciousness of having betrayed an authentic standard; it is the free judgement of the self by the self ... "False guilt" is that which comes as a result of the judgements and the suggestions of others. "True guilt" is that which results from Divine judgement.[20]

The remedy for true guilt is confession and forgiveness.[21] The answer to false guilt is a change of thinking and understanding. Many Christians are crippled by false guilt and often need help to "renew their minds",[22] and differentiate false from real guilt.

## Anger

When people become overwhelmed by feelings of worthlessness and inadequacy, they may become very angry. Anger is a *secondary emotion*. Sometimes it is so strong that it will obscure the precipitating emotion, in this case a feeling of failure. At other times, anger is not expressed outwardly but is buried, perhaps under feelings of self-pity. When a person is angry through a loss of self-worth, sometimes the anger is turned outwards and is expressed in aggressive behaviour. But very often the anger is turned inwards and results in self-destructive behaviour, such as over-eating, inactivity, drug dependency and sexual promiscuity. Self hatred can also lead to despair and suicide.

## Jealousy

If I do not love myself, I will assume that no one else will love me either. This can make it difficult for me to feel secure about another's love. I may see evidence of rejection by a friend where none was intended. A wife or husband with low self-esteem often feels unsure of their partner's love. If they see their partner relating well to another person – someone of the opposite sex, or even of the same sex, or perhaps to one of their own children – they will feel jealous. This will be interpreted as proof that their partner does not really love them as much. On the other hand, if people do love and feel good about themselves, they will be secure in their partner's love and will enjoy seeing their loved one relating well to someone else.

# RELATIONSHIP CONSEQUENCES OF POOR SELF-ESTEEM

Low self-esteem affects all our relationships: at school, at work, at home, at church. It is the cause of much loneliness and can inhibit our relationship with God.

Loneliness is possibly the most significant social problem of our time. Social isolation is in epidemic proportions in Western society, as more and more people have moved from rural to urban life during this century. "Loneliness is a mixed bag that has links to psychological, spiritual and social factors."[23]

Low self-esteem is sometimes a major part of the development of loneliness. If I do not feel good about myself, I will not want you to get close to me because you might find out what I am really like. So I will avoid real closeness at all costs. I may bury myself in my work, or sport, or hobbies, or even Christian activities – anything to distract me from the deep loneliness I feel. I could be outwardly gregarious with a lot of acquaintances, but may not be close to anyone. The real issue is how I feel about myself. This has been called "self-inflicted loneliness".[24] So if I find loneliness a problem, it would be important to assess how I really feel about myself.

## School

Childhood and adolescence can be very lonely. Studies in the United States have shown that young people have the most problems with loneliness, for a variety of reasons.[25] This is the period when people are most vulnerable to the effects of low self-esteem, as they search for identity and struggle for acceptance.

Often a young person tries to find the answer in an exclusive relationship with someone of the opposite sex. Researchers have found that one of the primary reasons adolescents get involved in premarital sex is that they have an unhealthy self-image.[26] They are looking for love and acceptance and substitute these with sex.

The self-concept that adolescents have determines so much of their behaviour. In a New Zealand study of adolescent girls, done for the Justice Department in 1972, it was found that a girl who thinks of herself as bad or a criminal is more likely than the girl who regards herself well to be involved in delinquent or criminal behaviour.[27]

## Work

A healthy self-esteem is basic to being able to develop good relationships at work. Not only is it one of your biggest assets to ensure success in any job, it also helps you to see workmates as colleagues rather than competitors. So often the workplace becomes the scene of intense competition and "one-upmanship". While this is usually equated with being smart, it can also be evidence of insecurity. Good self-esteem will greatly assist people to be successful in their work. In turn, their success will enhance their self-esteem.

## Family

The family should be a place where we can drop our "masks" and be real. But in many homes this is not so. The irony is that members of the family, especially the children, can usually see through our masks anyway! The problem starts when one or both parents have low self-esteem. This will ensure that they are in competition with one another, often putting each other down in order to try and make themselves feel better.

Parents who are unable to be real may set up a system of playing "*games*". The psychiatrist, Dr Eric Berne, who developed Transactional Analysis, coined this term. He defines a "game" as: "A set of transactions between people, which are superficially plausible but have a concealed motivation."[28] Such games are not fun. They are social interactions which are characterised by their ulterior quality and a psychological pay-off. People with low self-esteem ("Not OK" in Transactional Analysis terms) easily fall into the trap of game playing. If parents relate in this way, naturally children will copy the model set for them. The whole family can be locked into manipulating one another. Sometimes families need objective help from outside, such as family counselling, to restore healthy communication.

It is unlikely that permanent changes will take place unless members of the family address the issue of their own self-esteem. While psychological theories such as Transactional Analysis can be helpful in understanding human behaviour, often the core issue is not touched. "Something very deep is missing: the central issue of the terrible ache of the heart. Self-esteem is much more than changed behaviour."[29]

## Marriage

We have come across more lonely married people than lonely single people. A single person anticipates some degree of loneliness as part of being single. But most people assume that marriage will eliminate loneliness from their lives. *Marriage does not solve loneliness.* Being able to share my real self with another person is the only way to do this. Many married people are not able to share themselves with each other for a variety of reasons. The principle reasons are fear of rejection and the fear that my partner will not like me. If I do not like myself, I will certainly not risk that rejection. There can be no more desperate form of loneliness than to share the same house and bed with someone, but not to be able to share myself. Chekhov wrote: "If you are afraid of loneliness, don't marry!"

## Church

Another place where it ought to be safe to be real is in the Church family. Unfortunately, there is a temptation to put on our very best masks on Sundays. To be honest with fellow Christians about personal failings or needs might be seen as a "bad witness"! This reveals a need for a deeper level of honesty in our fellowships. Real sharing is possible when we are so moved by God's unconditional love for us and our worth to him, that we can risk vulnerability. Then we can be open and accountable to one another, building each other up in love.[30]

## Relationship with God

How we see ourselves also has a strong bearing on the quality of our relationship with God. If I see myself as worthless, then a real relationship with God, based on openness and honesty, is very difficult. If I am hiding behind masks in human relationships, in order to place myself in a good light, I will also be tempted to hide from God. Adam's first reaction after he sinned was to hide from God.[31] When Jesus came, he exposed the "game" that some religious leaders were playing both with people and with God, especially in their prayer life.[32]

But if I see myself as precious to God because I am made in his image and loved as part of his own family, then I can relate to him without fear. If I know I am totally forgiven as well as unconditionally loved by God, then I can feel fully accepted by him. As a result, I have nothing to hide. I do not need to play "games" with God any more, so I am free to develop a real and honest relationship with him.

The Bible is full of the message that we are of tremendous value to God. He wants us to know both *who we are,* and *who he is*, and longs for an intimate relationship with us. The blocks to this experience, even for deeply committed Christians, are often misunderstandings about who we are and what the Scriptures teach about God's view of us. This is expanded further in the next chapter.


# A LIFE PRINCIPLE

Jesus once stated a truth, which at first hearing sounds very unfair: "Whoever has will be given more, and he will have an abundance. Whoever does not have, even what he has will be taken from him."[33] We can apply this in many ways. For example: knowledge gives the capacity to acquire more knowledge. Solomon said: "Instruct a wise man and he will be wiser still; teach a righteous man and he will add to his learning." [34] Overcoming temptation makes us stronger next time we face that temptation. Giving in to temptation will ensure that we are weaker next time. Money invested wisely produces more money, but if used unwisely can cause bankruptcy.

These are obvious examples from everyday life, but this principle also applies to self-esteem. People with good self-esteem are likely to be successful in life and reap the benefits of this positive view of themselves and their world. They become "winners". On the other hand, people with poor self-esteem tend to become "losers", certainly in their relationships.

## SUMMARY

There are many inadequate behavioural compensations for a low self-esteem. These may bring temporary relief, but do nothing to change how people really feel about themselves. Low self-esteem can also have negative personal and relationship consequences. But we are not stuck with our self-esteem the way it is. *We can change*, with God's help and with determination. That is the message of the rest of this book.

# REFLECTIONS AND EXERCISES

1 Assess yourself on a score of 1 to 5 on each of the following twelve behaviours. The more honest you are the more useful will be the test

*Key for scoring*
1 = Mostly the first behaviour, 2 = Frequently the first, 3 = Midway, 4 = Commonly the second, 5 = Always the second.

| BEHAVIOUR | | YOUR SCORE |
|---|---|---|
| Excessively shy and retiring | outgoing and open | —— |
| Put myself down | accept myself | —— |
| Draw attention to myself | able to forget about myself | —— |
| Be the centre of attention | enjoy being one of a group | —— |
| Boast of my achievements | content, even if my achievements are not noticed | —— |
| Dogmatic in arguments | listen to others' views | —— |
| Suspicious of others | assume the best in others | —— |
| Rigid & fixed in my thinking | flexible in my thinking | —— |
| Aggressive in relationships | react assertively to others | —— |
| Driven by my work | enjoy my work, but not controlled by it | —— |
| Unable to say "No" | comfortable in saying "No" | —— |
| Hard to make relationships | make relationships easily | —— |
| | TOTAL | —— |

- Ask someone who knows you well, and cares about you, to do the same assessment of you. Then you can compare the two lists for a more balanced evaluation.
- What does this assessment say about your self-esteem?
- After completing the test see Note 35.

2 Reflect on the past week or two and try to identify whether you have used any of the preceding compensating behaviours. What do you think was

happening for you at the time? Was your self-esteem being threatened in any way? What was the purpose of the behaviour you chose? What would have been a better response to the situation?

3 Think back to the last time you remember being dogmatic or when you stuck rigidly to a point of view in an argument. Did you have the niggling feeling that you might, in fact, have been in the wrong? What were you really trying to defend?

- If you are in a group setting, share any of the above insights with the others.

4 Write in your journal things that you have felt guilty about in the past, and sort them into two lists under the headings:

**Real Guilt**: Things you have done which were against your moral convictions or what you know to be God's standard.

**False Guilt**: Things you have felt guilty about because of social pressures, being manipulated by others or because of the fear of losing the love of others.

- How much have the issues of "false guilt" hindered your life? What do you intend to do about them?
- There is value in discussing this issue of guilt in a safe group, or with an understanding friend, or counsellor.

5 If you have experienced depression (whether a depressive illness or just times when you felt a bit low), think about ways in which your "self talk" – made your depression worse, or – helped you to be free of it.

- It could be helpful to actually write down things that you say to yourself in times of depression, resolving to replace these with positive statements, if they are negative ones.

6 Reflect back on times of stress. How did you feel about yourself during those times?
   – Confident and positive
   – useless and inadequate?

   - Which of the above is your normal reaction under stress?
   - If you have experienced both reactions at times, which response was most associated with times in which you coped well with the stress?

7 We have all experienced times of loneliness. Sometimes we deal with it quite well and at other times we feel devastated. Think about times of loneliness you have known and how you were feeling about yourself at the time.

   - See if you can identify some correlation between the two.
   - Check out your experience with others in the group.

8 Think about the following as it applies to the family in which you grew up and the family where you now live;

   - How much were/are you able to be honest and real with each other?
   - How much manipulation took place (even for the kindest motives)?
   - What psychological "games" are involved?

9  How do you react in your church fellowship? Do you tend to wear your "successful Christian mask" most of the time, or are you able to be open and real with some people? Are you aware of any "games" being played in your church fellowship?

  • What does this say
    – about you?
    – about your church fellowship?

10 Reflect on how you really FEEL about God in the following aspects of your relationship. Score yourself on a continuum from 0–10 depending on which you feel (not think) is appropriate for you.

   10 = you experience the characteristic under "A" all the time,
   0 = you experience "B" all the time.

   You are likely to score somewhere between the two.

## I EXPERIENCE GOD AS:

| A | B | YOUR SCORE |
|---|---|---|
| Close and always present | Distant and detached | —— |
| Like a father/mother | Like a stranger | —— |
| Comforting and supportive | Cold and unsupportive | —— |
| Caring about my needs | My needs don't concern him | —— |
| Forgiving and pardoning | Unforgiving and judging | —— |
| My friend and companion | Impersonal and neutral | —— |
| Loving and tender | Angry and resentful | —— |
| Understanding and reasonable | Intolerant and impatient | —— |
| Fair and just | Unfair and cruel | —— |
| Interested in me personally | Not interested in me | —— |
| | TOTAL % | —— |

NOTE: Your total is a percentage representing the quality of your relationship with God, or at least, how you are feeling about him right now.

- Consider how your responses to the above might relate to:

  a) Your attitudes to yourself.
  b) Your experiences in childhood, especially in your relationship with your father and mother.
  c) Your concept of God.
  d) Your experience of God.
  e) A mixture of all of these.

- In the items where your experience relates strongly to the "B" side of the scale, ask the Lord to "re-parent" you so that you become aware of the "A" dimensions. Make this your daily reflection and prayer for a month. God longs for you to enjoy your relationship with him in these ways. Trust him to make this a reality and thank him for what he is doing in your life.

## FIVE

# TOWARDS A THEOLOGY OF SELF-ESTEEM

*A healthy self-image is seeing yourself as God
sees you – no more and no less.*[1]

Josh McDowell

Over the centuries, there has been controversy
and confusion in the Christian Church about
the concept of self-esteem. The issue is still very
much alive. The debate raises old arguments, such
as: predestination and free will; how much God is
responsible and how much we are responsible for
our personal growth and sanctification. With the
resurgence of New Age teaching and humanistic
philosophy – that man is in charge of his destiny and
can solve all his own problems – many Christians are
understandably wary of the topic of "self-esteem".
There is confusion even over the word "self" and also
over what the Bible means when it commands us to
"love yourself". This chapter aims to address these
issues and present a "theology of self-esteem".


## NEGATIVE TEACHING

Perhaps the book which has been read more than
any other by Christians since the fifteenth century,

apart from the Bible, is *The Imitation of Christ*, by Thomas à Kempis. This book contains excellent teaching which has been a blessing to many. But there are also some statements which promote a very negative view of self. For example:

> A man who really knows his own nature sets no value on himself . . . The highest and most profitable form of study is to understand one's inmost nature and despise it . . . If I condemn myself, utterly abase myself, abandon all self-esteem, treat myself as the dust that I am, then your grace will favour me . . . The right thing for me to think and say is this – Lord, *I am nothing*. I possess nothing good of myself but am deficient in everything, and my end is nothing. The more violence you do to yourself, the greater will be your growth in grace . . . Man must think of himself as he really is: *nothing* . . . Truly to know and *despise oneself* is the most perfect counsel. (Italics ours.)[2]

Statements such as these, coming from someone regarded as a saint, were accepted without question for many centuries. He may not have intended to give the impression of our abject worthlessness, but this is certainly the conclusion that many people have drawn from it. This attitude surfaces later in the writings of John Calvin, who speaks of self-love as a "pest".[3] He may well have been referring to the destructiveness of pride and self-centredness, but does not clarify this as distinct from healthy self-love.

This thinking appears also in some more modern devotional writings, for example:

Those who have been in tropical lands tell us
that there is a big difference between a snake
and a worm, when you attempt to strike at them.
The snake rears up and hisses and tries to strike
back – a true picture of self. But a worm offers no
resistance; it allows you to do what you like with
it, kick it or squash it under your heel – a picture
of true brokenness. Jesus was willing to become
just that for us – a worm and not a man. He did
so, because that is what he saw us to be, worms
having forfeited all rights by our sins, except to
deserve hell. And now he calls us *to be worms*
for him.[4]

This "worm" philosophy, or "Man is Muck" theology, as it is sometimes called, is very destructive
and *not consistent with Scripture*. Christ certainly
does not call us "to be worms for him" in any
true sense of the word. Worms were created by
God but they were not created in his image as we
are! The statement "I am a worm and not a man,
scorned by men and despised by the people",[5] was a
description of how David was treated by his enemies,
not a picture of how he saw himself. Psalm 22 is
also prophetic, depicting how the Messiah would
be treated about a thousand years later by the
Jews. But this certainly does not imply that Jesus
saw himself as a worm in the same way as his
murderers did thus providing a "worm model" for
us to follow.

One of Job's miserable comforters, Bildad, describes man as a "maggot – a son of man, who is
only a worm!"[6] Here again, this is clearly not a
definitive description of mankind, and God himself
said of Job's three friends that they "have not spoken
of me what is right".[7]

David described man very differently: "You made him a little lower than the heavenly beings and crowned him with glory and honour. You made him ruler over the works of your hands; you put everything under his feet."[8] The NIV footnote to this passage points out that it could equally well be translated "made him a little lower than God".

Again, the psalmist wrote: "I said, 'You are "gods"; you are all sons of the Most High.'"[9] Jesus took up this thought when talking to the Jews: "Is it not written in your Law, 'I have said you are gods'? If he called them 'gods', to whom the word of God came – and the Scripture cannot be broken – what about the one whom the Father set apart as his very own and sent into the world?"[10]

However we may interpret these passages, at least *they do not suggest that God considers man is muck*, a worm, or to be despised. Rather, that human beings were the pinnacle of his creation. The image of God in humanity was marred by sin, but through the salvation that Christ has provided, the effects of sin in our lives can be reversed.

The logic of the "Man is Muck" theology goes something like this:

1) We are sinners. (Romans 3:23)
2) Sin permeates the whole of our nature. (Romans 7:18)
3) Therefore we are totally depraved and have lost God's image.
4) Therefore we are worthless.

The individual will naturally interpret this thinking as follows:

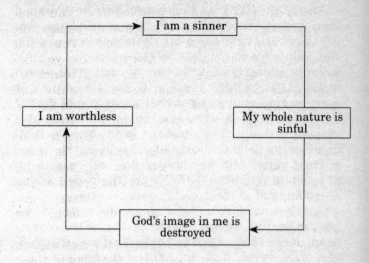

**Figure 3.** The 'Man is Muck' Theology Cycle.

The breakdown of the argument is between steps 2 and 3, and also between 3 and 4. It is true that we are sinners, and this has affected the whole of our unregenerate nature. But it is NOT true that sin has totally destroyed God's image in us. As Francis Schaeffer put it: "It is important to note that fallen man still retains something of the image of God. The Fall separates man from God, but it does not remove his original differentiation from other things."[11] To quote another theologian, A. H. Strong: "This natural likeness to God is *inalienable*, and as constituting a capacity for redemption, gives value to the life of even the unregenerate."[12] This is evident from what God said to Noah following the flood. After stating that "every inclination [of man's] heart is evil from childhood" (Genesis 8:21) he then reaffims that man is still "made in the image of God" (9:6).

Also, it is NOT true that because we have sinned therefore we are worthless. We are *unworthy but not worthless*, and there is a big difference between the two. While we do not deserve God's love and favour, we are recipients of it. We are of such great worth to God that he sent his Son to die for us, and it is preposterous to suggest that Jesus would die for something that is worthless. In fact, Jesus told a parable to help us understand our worth to him, in which he calls the kingdom of heaven the "pearl of great value". He was prepared to sell everything in order to purchase it.[13] We are the people of his kingdom, and of inestimable value to him.

God does not love us because we are worthy of his love, or because we can earn it. *God's love is unconditional.* It does not depend on the perfection or the goodness of the object loved, but on his perfection and goodness. He made this quite clear to his chosen people, the Jews: "The Lord did not set his affection on you and choose you because you were more numerous than other peoples ... But it was because the Lord loved you."[14] Paul reminds us that God's attitude is still the same: "God demonstrates his own love for us in this: While we were still sinners, Christ died for us."[15]

## EGO AND SARX

It is has often been taught that a person's "ego" is bad and that Christians must have their ego, or self, put to death and replaced by Christ if they are to grow in sanctification. This means that the real me must die, because it is tainted by sin and therefore of no worth. Of course, if I already have a poor self-image, I will readily believe that proposition, because

it fits in with what I think about myself anyway.[16]
Let us examine this line of theology.

## Word meanings

The Greek word "*ego*" simply means "I" (first person
pronoun, nominative) and occurs over 300 times in
the New Testament.[17] It is used by Christ and all the
apostles about themselves. It has no negative connota-
tion but denotes the entire person. For example,
Jesus said: "But I [*ego*], when I am lifted up from the
earth, will draw all men to myself [*emautos*]."[18]

Similarly, the Greek word "*automatos*" simply
means *self*, or "of oneself".[19] A clear example is
the verse just quoted, or another: "He himself bore
our sins."[20] In Scripture, "I" (ego) and "self" refer to
my *total person*, who I am, a person made in God's
likeness. They have no negative implications.

Another confusion has been between the use of
the word "*flesh*" in the literal and the metaphorical
senses. The Greek word "*sarx*" occurs 138 times in
the New Testament, usually referring to the human
body, or our flesh. It is also used metaphorically, for
example, in marriage, where the husband and wife
become "one flesh".[21] This refers to the process of
two people becoming one, through their growth in
intimacy – physically, emotionally and spiritually.

Paul also uses the word "sarx" in another way,
to denote *our sinful nature*, referring to the seat of
sin in humankind.[22] He says: "I know that nothing
good lives in me, that is, in my sinful nature", or as
the AV renders it: "I know that in me (that is, in my
flesh,) dwelleth no good thing."[23] Many people in the
past, and even today, think that this is saying that
my "ego" is totally bad, when clearly it is referring
to my sinful nature.

Another mistaken implication has been that our bodies (our "flesh") are of themselves bad. Paul's statement, just quoted, was taken by many in the early Church as a biblical justification of the prevailing Greek philosophy (Platonic thinking) that the spirit is essentially good and the body is evil. This was part of the Gnostic heresy of the early Church. Thus, early Christians believed they had to "mortify" themselves (put their flesh to death) by flagellating and abusing their bodies in the hope that this would improve their souls. Thomas à Kempis stated this in the passage quoted earlier. This teaching was a distortion of Paul's instructions that we should be in control of our bodies and not let them control us.[24]

This way of thinking is still common. I (John) was brought up to care for my body, but not to value it or respect it; to use it but not to enjoy it. From the teaching I was exposed to, I inferred that the body is suspect and of little value. Thus to enjoy physical pleasure in any form was decadent misuse of the body. It has taken me years to correct this distortion and accept that my physical body is created to be the "temple of the Holy Spirit"[25], which can be pleasing to God when given back to him.[26]

It is helpful to contrast the words "ego" and "sarx" in Scripture. Both are part of the real "me", but God's purpose for each of them is entirely different: my "*flesh*", or my sinful (carnal) nature is to be put to death,[27] because the "works of the flesh" are displeasing to God.[28] My selfishness and self-centredness are incompatible with a life that is controlled by the Spirit of God. My "*ego*", i.e. my personality and uniqueness, which Christ has redeemed, is to be handed over to him to be developed. My true self is good because it has been created by him, and as a little boy once said: "God don't make no junk!" His purpose for us is that we become mature, reaching

| **SARX\*** | **EGO\*** |
|---|---|
| 'Flesh' | 'I' |
| My sinful ('carnal') nature | My personality; real self |
| My self-centredness | My uniqueness |
| 'The works of the flesh' | My gifts and abilities |
| | |
| To decrease; be eliminated | To be developed |
| To be put to death | To be made alive |
| Displeasing to God | Pleasing to God |
| | |
| See - Romans 8:5-8 | See - Romans 8:9-11 |
| Colossians 3:5 | Colossians 3:10 |

\* 'Flesh' is used here in its metaphorical, not literal sense.

**Figure 4.** Contrasting the Meanings of 'Sarx' and 'Ego'

the "whole measure of the fulness of Christ".[29] The differences are summarised in figure 4.

## Hymnology

Negative reinforcement of our self-esteem has crept into some of the well-known hymns. Here are two examples: a) In that lovely old hymn: "Beneath the cross of Jesus", the 4th verse states:

> Two wonders I confess –
> The wonders of his glorious love,
> and *my own worthlessness*. (Italics ours.)

The dictionary defines "worthless" as: "Without worth, use or value; without moral worth, low and despicable."[30] Elizabeth Clephane may have intended the latter meaning in her hymn, but people would usually assume the first meaning, especially if they already felt that way about themselves. It must be stated clearly: We are *unworthy but not worthless*.

b) The "worm theology" gets apparent support from Isaac Watt's famous devotional hymn:

> Alas! And did my Saviour bleed?
> And did my Sovereign die?
> Would he devote that sacred head
> For such a worm as I?

# A BIBLICAL BASIS FOR GOOD SELF-ESTEEM

Josh McDowell gives an excellent definition of a healthy self-image: "*Seeing yourself as God sees you – no more and no less.*"[31] In Chapter 3 we pointed out that children discover who they are by seeing themselves the way others see them. The image they have of themselves is based on what is reflected back to them from the "mirror" that their parents and other significant adults provide. Similarly, as God's children, we derive our self-image and our sense of self-worth from the way God sees us. So it is very important that we get an accurate picture from the "mirror" of God's word. This mirror is not "cracked!"

# THE IMAGE OF GOD

The foundation of my self-image is the knowledge that I am created in the image of God. "God created man in his own image, in the image of God he created him; male and female he created them."[32] The writer believed the fact that we are created in God's image to be so important that he repeated the statement three times in two verses.

A person who does not know God, or who believes there is no God, still has to answer the existential question: "Where do I come from?", because we must come from somewhere. If I do not come from something higher, then I must come from something lower – perhaps an ape, or a tadpole! So, aside from the debate about whether or not the theory of evolution has scientific validity, ascent from lower animals becomes an essential part of the belief system of someone who does not acknowledge God, certainly in Western culture.

What then does it mean to be made in the image or likeness of God? Clearly, we cannot reflect the image of God in the same way as Christ did as the Son of God on earth.[33] Nor does the term merely imply physical form. The physical characteristics of our bodies are very similar to other animals, some of which are more efficient in certain areas than we are: a horse can run faster, an eagle can see better, a dog has more acute hearing. In terms of our physical bodies we are no more godlike than a rabbit or a cat.

The "image of God" refers to the *divine qualities* with which we have been endowed. These set humanity apart from the rest of creation. The following are some of these qualities:

## The ability to relate

God lives in relationship; Father, Son and Holy Spirit. Hence the plural pronouns: "Let *us* make

man in *our* image" (italics ours).[34] God has made
us with a similar capacity and need to relate, both
to him and to our fellow human beings. The desire
we have for companionship is shared with most
other creatures, but the degree to which humans
are capable of relationship is unique. The quality
of our lives depends largely on the quality of our
relationships.

## Intelligence

God has created us with the ability to think, reason,
see ourselves objectively and solve problems, to an
extent that is far superior to the rest of creation.
We are not all-knowing as God is, but the power of
the human mind is awesome – a power which can be
used for good or evil.[35]

## The ability to make choices

We have been given a will and can take responsibility
for our lives.[36] Our decisions can be based on rational
thought and will, not limited to instinct or learned
behaviour like the rest of the animal world, though
we can still be influenced strongly by such factors.
Our "free" wills have been biased by sin but we can
still make choices.

## The capacity to love

Human beings often love imperfectly, but they are
capable of tremendous heights of love and altru-
ism.[37] Love is the most powerful force in the world.
The more fully we are living our lives in God, the
more he enlarges our capacity to love. The more we
give love, the more our love grows.

## *The ability to be creative*

God is the Creator, and has given human beings the capacity to be creative too, with our minds and hands. He also gave us the privilege of being able to co-create new lives.

## *Our spiritual dimension*

This is the most significant way in which we are made in God's image. He has made us spiritual beings, created with the capacity for relationship with him. It is this which sets the human race apart from the rest of creation and without a relationship with God we are not fully human.

These gifts and attributes are as amazing as they are humbling. But we must grasp that being created in the image of God is the foundation of our self-worth. As Bruce Narramore puts it so well:

> Our identity begins with the fact that we are image-bearers. Only secondarily do we have to account for the sin that entered man's perfect state. This point is exceedingly important. As we erect a basis for our identity, we can look at one of two conditions. We can either look *first* at our sinfulness, and erect a basically negative self-image, or we can look *first* to our divine origin and destiny and then build an essentially positive self-concept. (Italics ours.)[38]

We have thought of the divine qualities with which we have been endowed. Now consider the amazing "machine": The human body.

# THE WONDER OF ME

As a nurse and a doctor, we have been privileged to study and to care for human bodies for over forty years. We still never cease to be amazed at the body's incredible design. It is so easy to take its construction for granted. The following are just a few marvellous facts about our bodies.[39]

We have minds that can think at 800 words a minute and have an almost unlimited memory capacity. Our eyes contain 127,000,000 light receptor cells which transmit the messages received along about one million nerve fibres to the brain where an accurate picture is recorded. This is no easy task, as the brain has to sort out approximately one billion messages a second which it receives from the retinae of the eyes alone. Our ears are equally wonderful precision instruments. They contain 25,000 sound reception cells, tuned to different vibration frequencies, and the ear can distinguish approximately 300,000 separate tones. These are changed from mechanical to electrical energy to be transmitted to the brain.

The brain receives and sorts out billions of messages at once both from the outside world and from within the body. They travel via seven miles of nerve fibres. Messages from within include information about posture and balance as well as data from more than half a million touch-detectors in the skin. Then there is a mass of data from the autonomic nervous system that controls the internal organs of the body.

To service the machine, the human heart pumps about 2000 gallons of blood around 60,000 miles of blood vessels each day. Each red cell lasts three to four months and does half a million round trips in that time in order to bring oxygen to the cells of the body. The bone marrow produces one million red cells per second to replace worn out ones.

The blood also carries many other things, such as, food to provide the body with energy; nutrients for growth and repair of the tissues; white cells ("soldier" cells) and antibodies to fight off invading germs; hormones to convey messages to various organs. At the same time it removes waste products from worn out tissues and from muscle action.

The more we know of the body the more we marvel at its construction and can only acknowledge the skill of the Designer. The Greek playwright Sophocles, in the fifth century BC, declared the human body to be "the most wondrous of the world's wonders". Five centuries earlier, King David acknowledged both the Creator and the beauty of his creation, when he exclaimed: "For all these mysteries I thank you: for the wonder of myself for the wonder of your works."[40] The literal Hebrew translation can be rendered: "I thank you Lord that I am wonderful."

# HOW GOD SEES US

The place to start is to discover how much God loves us. When you really love someone you will see her/him in a totally different light from the way others see that person. It is often said that "love is blind". That is not true. Infatuation is blind, but *true love is far-sighted*. True love sees in another person what the eye without love cannot see. The loved one is of great value to us and the greater our love the more valuable the loved one becomes.

Also, real love sees loved ones not only as they are
but *as they can become*. And this is certainly how
God sees us.

The predominant message of the Bible is that God
loves us. St Augustine said: "The Bible contains our
love-letters from home." For example:

- God has loved us *from the beginning*: "I have
  loved you with an everlasting love; I have drawn
  you with loving-kindness."[41]
- God loves us *now*: "How great is the love the
  Father has lavished on us, that we should be
  called children of God!"[42]
- God's love for us extends *to the future*: "No
  eye has seen, no ear has heard, no mind has
  conceived what God has prepared for those who
  love him."[43]

Jesus told us something of the extent to which we
are loved by God. It is truly mind-boggling. In his
prayer to his Father he says: "You . . . have loved
them even as you have loved me."[44] This means
that God loves us in the same way that he loves
his Son, Jesus. In talking to the disciples, the Lord
said: "As the Father has loved me, so I have loved
you."[45] In other words, Jesus is saying that he loves
his followers to the same degree that his Father
loves him!

How can we grasp this? It is very difficult indeed.
Fortunately, God has given us his Holy Spirit to help
us comprehend this truth: "We are able to hold our
heads high no matter what happens and know that
all is well, for we know how dearly God loves us,
and we feel this warm love everywhere within us
because God has given us the *Holy Spirit to fill our
hearts with his love*" (italics ours).[46] *God's love is*

*totally unconditional.* We do not deserve it and can
do nothing to earn it. It is God's gift to us. Many
people find this hard to accept. It is easy to become
like the elder brother in the story of the prodigal son.
Angry at his father for still loving the rebel who had
wasted the family fortune on riotous living, he was
not even able to enjoy his own blessings. The elder
son could not accept the love he was being offered
too. At the end of the parable the father says: "My
son, you are always with me, and everything I have is
yours."[47] The tragedy was, he did not really believe
it. All he could do was complain that he had never
been given one of the farm goats, which he owned
anyway, to throw a party for his friends!

The problem may not be so much that we have a
small view of ourselves, but *we have a small view
of God*. We cannot comprehend that God can be so
incredibly loving and generous. David, in the well
known Psalm 23, expressed an understanding of
God's generosity and love that we would do well
to absorb. "You prepare a table before me in the
presence of my enemies. You anoint my head with
oil; my cup overflows" (v 5).

He is not just saying here that God provides food
for him in difficult circumstances, but he tells us
how he experiences the way God sees him, as the
*special guest*. The Good News Bible translates this
sentence as: "You welcome me as an honoured guest
and fill my cup to the brim." This captures the true
sense of the passage. In the culture of that day, the
honoured guest was anointed with oil on arrival at
dinner. A slave was assigned to stand behind him to
keep filling up his cup with wine, whenever it was
partly empty. This represents how God treats those
who know him as their Shepherd.

*Do you believe it?* When people have been put

down all their lives and have come to believe that they are "worthless", a huge shift in their thinking is needed. Their vision of themselves and their vision of God both have to change. God has given us his Holy Spirit to make it happen, but we also have to be part of the process. It has taken us personally a long time to grasp this truth and we are still working on it. The Lord in his grace can transform our thinking.

Here is how a friend of ours came to rely on God's love, despite her negative circumstances. Joanna was born into a Christian home, but her mother was a very neurotic person. During her pregnancy with Joanna, she felt a lot of uterine pains. This convinced her that there was something wrong with her baby and that it would be born deformed. Despite her mother's predictions, Joanna was born a healthy child. However, her mother refused to believe this and all through her childhood Joanna was regarded by her parents as abnormal. She was given a variety of weird and degrading treatments by unqualified charlatans. She was also sexually abused by her father.

Joanna obediently accepted all this, having been taught that parents can't be wrong and must be obeyed. In spite of this background and the medical problems that followed the so-called "treatment", Joanna grew up with a healthy self-esteem. Two factors were responsible for this. One was the unconditional love she received from her grandmother, who believed in her and affirmed her. The other was her strong faith and the conviction that she was accepted and loved by God unconditionally.

When people have missed out on unconditional love in their growing up years, it is essential for them to have a new vision of what Yahweh is like.

As we absorb the truth of the word of God, we can be *re-parented* and bask in God's all-embracing love. This process seldom happens instantaneously and may take a long time. That is why God took the trouble to write a lengthy love-letter to us. Just as a lover reads and re-reads a letter from his or her beloved to absorb the message, so we need to do this with the Scriptures.

## GOD'S LOVE LETTER TO US

In Chapter 3 we described the Four As to summarise the positive influences that build self-esteem in children:

| | |
|---|---|
| Attention, | Acceptance, |
| Affirmation, | Affection. |

In Scripture, we can identify these four As, which portray God's attitude to us, his children. Their truth can build our self-esteem.

### Attention

God's attention to us and love for us actually starts *before birth*: "My frame was not hidden from you when I was made in the secret place. When I was woven together in the depths of the earth, your eyes saw my unformed body. All the days ordained for me were written in your book before one of them came to be."[48] In this poetic way, David describes how God is interested in us from conception to birth. So it is logical for David to say in the same psalm that God is interested in all the details of our lives now:

> You know when I sit or stand. When far away
> you know my every thought. You chart the path
> ahead of me, and tell me where to stop and rest.
> Every moment, you know where I am. You know
> what I am going to say before I even say it. You
> both precede and follow me, and place your hand
> of blessing on my head.[49]

Some people think of God's watchful eye on us as
that of a tyrant, checking to see if we get out of
line in order to punish us. That is not the picture
at all. God loves us so much that he can't take his
eyes off us, in the same way that a loving human
parent will gaze with love and tenderness at their
little child.

The Bible leaves us in no doubt about the fact
that God knows us individually, even *by name*.
God, speaking through Isaiah to Israel said: "Fear
not, for I have redeemed you; I have called you by
name; you are mine" and "See, I have engraved you
on the palms of my hands."[50] Jesus, in describing
himself as the Shepherd with his flock, says of us:
"He calls his own sheep by name and leads them
out."[51] To help us understand the degree to which
our Heavenly Father knows us and cares for us,
Jesus said: "Even the very hairs of your head are
all numbered"![52]

Probably there is no more sensitive part of the
body than the eye. So Zechariah uses this metaphor
to describe how precious we are to God: "Whoever
touches you touches the apple of his eye."[53] God
treats people with as much care as a person would
give to his eyesight.

Experts in comparative religion have identified significant differences between Christianity and other
faiths. Almost every doctrine of Christian theology

is replicated in one form or another, even if grossly distorted, by other religions. But there are some major differences:

- Many religions describe human beings in their search for a god who is "out there" – unknown and unknowable. Christianity claims that *God took the initiative* in searching for humanity in general and people as individuals.[54]
- In the other great faiths, people are not significant and the individual is just part of the mass of humanity. The message of the Bible is that *the individual is important* and that God desires a relationship with each one of us, because of his great love for us.

It was this truth that transformed St Paul, when he finally discovered "the Son of God, who loved me and gave himself for me".[55] We can all claim this truth for ourselves, that Christ loved me and died for me. This establishes beyond doubt the individual's worth to God. "God's whole plan for humankind is built on the assumption that we are significant to him."[56]

## Acceptance

We are fully accepted by God, in Christ. "He hath made us accepted in the beloved."[57] This is referring to the way we have been adopted into God's family through Jesus Christ and clothed in his righteousness. Peter took a while to learn that this acceptance is not exclusive but is open to all. He said: "I now realise how true it is that God does not show favouritism but accepts men from every nation who fear him and do what is right."[58] In turn, we are to accept others *because* we have been accepted by God.

"Accept one another, then, just as Christ accepted you."[59]

*Affirmation*

God affirms us in so many ways. To cite just a few examples:

- God *listens to us*. To listen to people means to value and respect them. When I am really listened to I feel affirmed and loved. We are told many times in Scripture that God listens to us. "I love the Lord, for he heard my voice" . . . "This is the confidence we have in approaching God: that if we ask anything according to his will, he hears us."[60]

- God is willing to enter into *dialogue with us*.[61] There are many examples in Scripture of this: Abraham, Moses, Job, Nicodemus, the Samaritan woman, to name a few.[62] To discuss something with someone is a tacit affirmation that the one we are talking with is valued.

- God regards us as *his friends*. In the Old Testament, only two great men, Abraham and Moses, were called friends of God.[63] But the good news is that, in Christ, God regards US as his friends: "We were God's enemies, but he made us his friends through the death of his Son. Now that we are God's friends, how much more will we be saved by Christ's life!"[64]

- God has *adopted us into his family*.[65] He has also given us the full rights and privileges of children of his family. "God sent his Son . . . to redeem those under law, that we might receive the full rights of sons [and daughters] . . . So you are no longer a slave, but a son; and since you are a son, God has made you also an heir."[66] There could hardly be a greater affirmation of who we are in God's sight than this: God has made us his children, both by creation and redemption. "Now you are no longer strangers to God and foreigners to heaven, but you are members of God's very own family, citizens of God's country, and you belong in God's household with every other Christian."[67]

*Affection*

*God loves us*. We have already described the wonder of his love for us. This was something that Paul emphasised again and again in his letters:

> May your roots go down deep into the soil of God's marvellous love; and may you be able to feel and understand, as all God's children should, how long, how wide, how deep, and how high his love really is; and to experience this love for yourselves, though it is so great that you will never see the end of it or fully know or understand it.[68]

But perhaps the clearest way to understand God's attitude towards us is to see the way Jesus related to people.

# HOW JESUS TREATED PEOPLE

Jesus Christ came into the world to show us what God is like. The Bible tells us that Jesus was the "visible likeness of the invisible God".[69]

Therefore the way Jesus treated people must represent the attitude that God has to us all. The biography of Jesus in the Gospels provides many examples of how Jesus related to people.

- Jesus *accepted* and received people as they were and saw them as they could become. He accepted sinners, though not their sin. An ancient Persian proverb puts it: "There is no saint without a past; no sinner without a future." Jesus went out of his way to associate with needy people. He chose to spend time with publicans and sinners.[70]

- Jesus treated all people with *respect*, even the marginalised and despised ones. A classic example of this is how Jesus related to the woman at the well, who was not only a woman but a Samaritan.[71] He cut across barriers of gender and race to talk to her, which amazed the disciples. He even discussed theological issues, listening to her and answering her questions. Other men had used her, but here was a man who treated her with dignity and respect. No wonder she responded to his message!

- Jesus built up people's *self-worth*. Just one week before Calvary, Jesus took the time to spend a few hours with the most despised man in Jericho.[72] He chose to walk through the streets of the city with little Zacchaeus, who must have felt ten feet tall that day! It is not surprising that his life was changed.

- Jesus *did not condemn* people.[73] One day, they brought to him a woman "taken in adultery".[74] The Pharisees had already condemned her and were ready to stone her to death. After they had all gone, Jesus said to the woman: "Neither do I condemn you; go and sin no more." He clearly judged her behaviour, but she did not feel condemned as a person. He treated her with dignity and respect. Another time, a woman of the streets anointed his feet with perfume and her own tears while he was attending a feast. The host, Simon the Pharisee, saw her as a "sinner" – just a common prostitute. Jesus referred to her with respect as "this woman" – a woman who "loved much".[75]

These stories are not only recorded as a model for us to follow in the way we should treat people, but are a living demonstration of how God treats us. "Christ sometimes looked on people with anger, but never looked upon them with contempt."[76] None of us have ever been cherished, loved and valued by people in the way God cherishes, loves and values us. As we ponder these truths and allow the Holy Spirit to impress them upon our minds and hearts, so we learn to see ourselves as God sees us. This provides a firm foundation for good self-esteem.

St Paul makes some amazing statements about our value and worth to God: "Because of what Christ has done we have become gifts that God delights in . . . I want you to realize that God has been made rich because we who are Christ's have been given to him!"[77] How sad that we often devalue ourselves when this is how God values us. It is only when we discover our worth to God that we can have the courage to love ourselves.


## LOVE YOURSELF

Jesus said: "'Love the Lord your God with all your heart and with all your soul and with all your mind.'

This is the first and greatest commandment. And the second is like it: 'Love your neighbour as yourself.'"[78] Loving your neighbour as you love yourself was a command given by God to Moses 1500 years earlier,[79] reinforced by Jesus, re-stated in three of Paul's epistles and also by James.[80]

Unfortunately, many of us have learned to despise ourselves, some even to *hate* ourselves. We are aware of our failure to live up to God's standards, and our inability to love. Like Paul, we can say: "I do not understand what I do. For what I want to do I do not do, but what I hate I do . . . What a wretched man I am!"[81] We start by hating the things we *do*, that are against our better judgement, and end up hating and condemning *ourselves*. This self-rejection can be easily reinforced by the faulty theology we described earlier in the chapter. Remember that Satan is our "accuser"[82], not the Holy Spirit. Let us not join Satan in his destructive work.

Some Christians never get past the bondage of Romans chapter 7 and so never move on to the freedom of chapter 8: "Therefore, there is now no condemnation for those who are in Christ Jesus, because through Christ Jesus the law of the Spirit of life set me free from the law of sin and death."[83] It becomes almost a virtue for some people to hate themselves. In spite of what Jesus said they find it impossible, if not sacrilegious, to consider loving themselves.

Another problem is the fact that the word "love" is probably the most confused word in the English language. The word can mean to love deeply or to merely fancy something. A person can say, "I love my wife", and also, "I love ice cream". There is, or should be, a big difference between these two uses of the word love! Love can also be used to express lust. The word love is also used when we mean pride. "Doesn't he love himself!" implies that we think that person is very proud.

To love yourself, in the true sense, means to *respect, honour, value, cherish, esteem, care for yourself.* This describes good self-esteem. Selfishness and self-love are not the same thing; in fact, they are *opposites*. People who love themselves can forget about themselves and love others. People who do not love themselves are so preoccupied with the pain within that they become self-centred and selfish.

*Paul defines these two classes of people* with great clarity:

a) Describing selfish people who love themselves in the wrong sense, he wrote:

> People will be lovers of themselves, lovers of money, boastful, proud, abusive, disobedient to their parents, ungrateful, unholy, without love, unforgiving, slanderous, without self-control, brutal, not lovers of the good, treacherous, rash, conceited, lovers of pleasure rather than lovers of God."[84]

b) By contrast, people who are freed from their sinful nature can love themselves and others: "You, my brothers, were called to be free. But do not use your freedom to indulge the sinful nature; rather, serve one another in love. The entire law is summed up in a single command: 'Love your neighbour as yourself.'"[85] This truth is explored further in Chapter 8.

So, it is a *package deal*: love your neighbour AS yourself. One is not complete without the other. These ideas on self-love were expressed well by the thirteenth-century mystic, theologian and philosopher, Meister Eckhart:

If you love yourself, you love everybody else as you do yourself. As long as you love another person less than you do yourself, you will not really succeed in loving yourself. But if you love all alike, including yourself, you will love them as one person, and that person is both God and man.[86]

The person who does not love himself finds *pride* a great temptation. The person who loves herself can set herself aside and value and affirm another. Paul said: "In lowliness of mind let each esteem other better than themselves."[87] Clearly, I can only esteem you "better than myself", i.e. treat you with greater honour, respect and esteem if I honour, respect and esteem myself first. You cannot give to others what you do not have yourself.

Jesus modelled this principle for us at the Last Supper, recorded in John 13:3–17. The disciples were so preoccupied with an argument as to which of them was the greatest,[88] that none of them was able to take the humble place of the absent slave and wash the others' feet. They could not even bring themselves to wash Jesus' feet! It seems that their self-esteem was so low that all they could do was compete for prominence, like little children.

Then John tells us something very important about the Lord: "Jesus knew that the Father had put all things under his power, and that he had come from God and was returning to God" (v 3). In other words he had *perfect self-esteem*: he knew who he was, where he had come from and where he was going. The very next statement is: "So he got up from the meal, took off his outer clothing, and wrapped a towel round his waist. After that, he poured water into a basin and began to wash his disciples' feet, drying them with the towel." Jesus was able to be naturally humble because he had no problem with his sense of self-worth. He was not pretending to be their humble servant. He knew exactly who he was: their "Lord and Teacher" (v 14). "I have set you an example," said Jesus, "that you should do as I have done for you." As we deal with our low self-worth, so the fruit of humility has room to grow in us, and pride no longer has a place.

Learning to love yourself in the right way is a *life-long task*. But as we learn to love that which God loves so dearly – OURSELVES – so we will be free to love others more effectively and, indeed, to love God more fully.

# WHAT JESUS TAUGHT ABOUT SELF

Jesus not only told us to love others as we love ourselves, he also said: "If anyone would come after me, he must *deny* himself and take up his cross and follow me. For whoever wants to save his life will lose it, but whoever loses his life for me will find it" (emphasis ours).[89] Jesus taught this and also modelled it in his own life here on earth. William Barclay calls this statement the "recipe for life, as distinct from existence".[90] This is what life is all about: to deny myself and to lose my life for Christ's sake in order to find it.

Only people who fully love themselves, i.e. value, respect and esteem themselves, can fully deny themselves. The person who doesn't love herself or himself *sees nothing of worth to deny*. This is one of the reasons why so many Christians have never taken this step of denying themselves. It would be meaningless to deny something that you hate or think is worthless! To deny myself means to set aside any selfish claim of ownership or rights. As stated above, we belong to God by right of creation and redemption. Denying myself affirms this.

Some of the Christian teaching which I (Agnes) received in my youth centred around "denying self", "dying to self" and "crucifying self" by taking up my cross daily. The ultimate in following Jesus seemed to me to be not Christian living but Christian dying! During those years I was emerging from a shy child to a teenager lacking in confidence. I did not really like who I was, though I wanted to be someone for God. So this teaching about dying to self only served to reinforce the attitude I had towards myself.

Fortunately, I learned the real sense of God's love for me from my parents and this helped me overcome my lack of self-worth. When I discovered who I was in Christ, I was able to accept that he had created me to be someone of worth. Realising this helped me put into perspective the earlier teaching on dying, which I had been using as an excuse for not learning how to live. I appreciate now that denying self is a lifelong process, worked out in day-to-day living for Christ.

Psychiatrist M. Scott Peck expressed this well: "It is in the giving up of self that human beings can find the most ecstatic and lasting, solid, durable joy of life. And it is death that provides life with meaning. This 'secret' is the central wisdom of religion."[91]

*To lose my life* for Christ means that my life revolves around Christ and not self, for his glory, not mine.[92] It also means to give up security in material things and relinquish ultimate control of my life to him. It may even mean to lay aside the right to life itself. But people who risk all, and maybe appear to have lost all for Christ, find life. Soon after Jesus spoke these words, many Christians did lose their lives, literally. And the same is true today in some

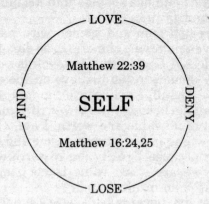

**Figure 5.** Summary of Jesus' Teaching About Self

parts of the world. But we have Jesus' word for it that when we lose anything for him we are more than amply rewarded.[93]

*Finding life* means discovering the meaning of life and the joy of living. Jesus said: "I have come that they may have life, and have it to the full."[94] Fullness of life means becoming the person I was created to be. St Francis of Assisi defined this paradox beautifully: "It is in dying that we are born again to eternal life." Our Lord's teaching about self is summarised in Figure 5:

## SUMMARY

Scripture asserts that human beings are made in the image of God. That image has been spoiled by sin, but not removed. God sees us of great worth and value, and loves us more than we can comprehend. He calls us his friends and has adopted into his family those who put their faith in Christ.

Jesus treated men and women with respect and dignity, even notorious sinners. In so doing he accurately reflected God's attitude towards us, and he ultimately demonstrated his love on the cross. If I do not love myself, *I am refusing to love something that Jesus loved enough to die for.* If I continue to see myself of no value and worth, I am telling God that he is wrong in his estimate of me and has made a mistake because I really am a worthless worm. "Insisting we are of no value is not simply false modesty, it is an insult to God."[95]

"The first step towards self love is a simple one. We need to make a conscious decision to see ourselves through the eyes of the Divine Lover."[96] Those who accept, love, value and esteem themselves are freed from self preoccupation and the pain of low self-esteem. They can go on to deny themselves. They can respond in love to God and truly love others. In losing their lives they find life.

# REFLECTIONS AND EXERCISES

1 Make a list in your journal of all the people who love you.

- Try to identify the particular way each one shows their love for you.
- What is it about you that each one loves and admires?

2 From reading the Psalms it is clear that David had excellent self-esteem. Read Psalm 139 and note all the things that David said about God that affirmed his self-esteem. How many can you identify with?

- Repeat this exercise with Psalm 23.
- Share your observations with your group.

3 Reflect on the ways that we have been created in God's image listed in this chapter. Try to think of some other ways we reflect his likeness. Thank God for the ways he has made you in his image.

4 Spend a few moments studying your hands.

- Notice their firmness and strength; their softness and gentleness.
- Become aware of the texture of the skin; its colour and warmth.
- Observe the sensitive movements and dexterity of your fingers, acting under your control.
- Marvel at their sensitivity to touch. Shut your eyes and become aware of all that your fingers can tell you as you touch the objects

around you. Touch another's hand and discover new ways to communicate with that person through touch.

- Pause to praise God for the marvels of his creation.

5 Stand unclothed in front of a full-length mirror. Look carefully at each part of your body: hair, face, neck, torso, back, arms and legs, etc. Appreciate their shape, symmetry, texture, gracefulness and sheer beauty. Thank God for the wonder of you!

- If you are married, repeat this exercise with your husband or wife present. Ask him or her to comment on what he or she finds especially attractive about each part of you. Do this for each other. Then together, thank God for the beauty of his handiwork.

6 Read slowly the story of the Prodigal Son (Luke 15:11–32). You may find it helpful to read it in a number of versions.

- Which of the characters do you identify with most? Perhaps you can see something of all of them in your experience of life.
- Note all the ways the Father offered *both* sons his unconditional love. Write them down in your journal and reflect on them. Are there any changes in your attitudes to yourself or to God that you might make as a result of your meditation?
- Share your observations in your group.

7 Reflect on some of the biblical statements in the section: "God's love letter to us" (page 107). For example, how does it affect you to know that:

God knows you by name and regards you as
his friend?
God listens to you and is willing to engage
in dialogue with you?
He has adopted you into his family and has
made you an heir?
God loves you as much as he loves Jesus?

* How does this make you *feel* about *God* and
  about *yourself*?

8 We have seen from Scripture that God has accepted
us as we are and that likewise we should accept
others.[97]

* Think of someone you find it hard to accept.
  What does your attitude to *that person* say
  about *you*?

9 Look at your face in the mirror for a moment.
Then say out loud to yourself: "God loves you and
I love you, . . . . . . ." (Use your first name here) Do
this every day for a week.

* Discuss your experience of this exercise with
  the your group.

10 Read again the section: "What Jesus taught about
self" (on pages 117–119)

* To what extent do you think that you love
  yourself?
* Have you taken seriously the command to
  deny yourself?
* To what degree have you been able to lose your
  life for Christ and . . . so to find it?

# PART 2

# GROWING IN SELF-ESTEEM

In Part 1 we defined good and poor self-esteem and explored ways in which our self-concept develops. We then considered how God sees us and defined a biblical basis for good self-esteem. In Part 2 we will describe ways in which we can develop a more healthy self-esteem.

**Chapter 6** presents the assumption that we are responsible for our self-esteem; that our self concept is consequent on the choices we make. We can examine and challenge the beliefs we have about ourselves, and change destructive "tapes" that play in our minds. A process for doing this is described.

**Chapter 7** Before we can make significant changes we need to understand ourselves. We are essentially two people: the "person" (my real self) and the "personage" (my self-picture). Growing in self-esteem means becoming real, genuine and authentic. Here we look at blocks to becoming real as well as ways of growing in reality and bringing the "person" and the "personage" closer together.

**Chapter 8** Once I know who I am, I must learn to accept and love myself, beginning with my body and including my strengths and weaknesses. It is hard to accept the things we don't like about ourselves, and ways of doing this are described. This helps us to be able to love ourselves as God loves us.

**Chapter 9** True self-acceptance enables you to be yourself authentically. This involves establishing

your identity clearly and learning to celebrate your
uniqueness. Who you are is more important than
what you do. We look at practical issues such as
learning to speak for yourself; becoming an "actor",
not a "reactor"; developing healthy assertiveness.

**Chapter 10** The most practical way of growing in
self-esteem is to reveal yourself to at least one
other person. Many people have never done this
and continue to hide behind "masks" or live inside
their "castles". We look at ways of dealing with these
masks and how to come out from our "safe refuges"
to really meet others. The process of revealing yourself through emotional dialogue is described. People
with healthy self-esteem are able to achieve satisfying relationships and to express their faith more
effectively.

# SIX

# TAKING RESPONSIBILITY FOR YOUR SELF-ESTEEM

*Now choose life, so that you and your
children may live.[1]*

Moses c. 1450 BC

God has created us with the ability to make choices. God chose to love us and he wants us to choose to love him. He did not create a race of robots programmed to make the right decisions, but beings like himself who would respond to him in love and relate to him by choice. Moses developed this kind of relationship with God and wanted the Israelites to pursue it too. After leading them for forty years he set before the people two options: life and prosperity, or death and destruction. The former would follow as they loved and obeyed the Lord and the latter would be the result of turning away from God. He also pointed out that the consequences of their choice would affect their children.

So it is with us. We have a choice which determines the quality of our lives. While it may not affect our eternal destiny, it does affect the quality of our living and our relationships here and now. As was described in Chapter 3, the level of self-esteem that parents have strongly influences what their children's will be like as they discover their own identity.

Whether they are aware of it or not, parents are the
models children use to build their lives. Fortunately,
each child also has the power of *choice*. Children
brought up by parents with a poor self-esteem may
initially copy that life style, but can choose later
in life to be different. Change is difficult but it
is possible. Life is composed of a healthy balance
between two complementary principles. On the one
hand we acknowledge God's grace in our lives, and
on the other hand that we are responsible for our
own happiness and joy. "To be free people we must
assume total responsibility for ourselves."[2] This is
true from childhood, even for someone who has had
a disadvantaged background.[3] Assuming responsibility for our attitudes and behaviour is essential
before any growth can take place. So the first step
in improving my self-esteem is to take responsibility
for it and acknowledge that I can do something about
it. I am able to make some significant changes which
will alter the way I see myself and how I feel about
myself. I will probably need some help from others
and particularly from God. But *they cannot do it for
me*. I have to make the changes myself.


# THINGS THAT PREVENT US MAKING
# CHANGES

Why is it then that some people can be very much
aware of their low self-image and exceedingly uncomfortable because of their lack of self-esteem, but do
nothing about it? How is it that some people want to
be free of this burden of feeling inferior, yet continue
to allow others, even members of their own family,
to put them down? What stops people from making

changes and what prevents growth? The following are some of the reasons why we may not make changes, even when aware of the need.

## Fear of change

All change is threatening. To change a pattern of behaviour, which I may have used since childhood to cope with the harsh realities of life, is scary. Even if I am aware that it is an inadequate response to the situation, at least it is one that I am familiar with. As the old proverb expresses it: "Better the devil you know than the one you don't!"

John Powell puts it this way:

> We look for *predictability*. Knowing what to expect gives us a sense of security. It enables us to make decisions about how to act. Soon our own actions fall into patterns which are based on our perceptions and adjustments to reality. Life becomes predictable, and our actions take on consistency. We are usually willing to act well or badly to maintain this consistency. The opposite of predictability is *chaos*. Chaos boggles the mind and fragments the spirit.[4]

So, reluctance to change usually reflects a desire to play it safe. But in order to change wrong perceptions about ourselves and about our world we must be prepared to take the risk of some turbulence in our lives.

Many people are aware of their low self-esteem and may seek counselling to help them deal with this. Some are willing and ready to implement changes in their lives. Others just want life to be a little more comfortable for them, but are not prepared to challenge their faulty thinking or self-defeating behaviour. They resemble a man standing in a muddy ditch with only his nose and mouth out of water.

Someone on the bank calls out to him: "Let me help you on to dry land. The sun is shining up here." "No thanks," he replies, "I might slip in again. Actually, it's quite warm down here, and at least my feet are on the bottom. But I'd be grateful if you'd stop anyone from making waves, so I can continue to breathe!" So it is with some people who do not like themselves but are afraid to do anything about it. They often do not want to make real changes in their lives, they just want help to be a bit more comfortable the way they are. Helplessness can become a habit.

## Learned helplessness

This is a neurotic way of dealing with the problem of low self-esteem, but some people have discovered how powerful it is to be weak. For example, when you are helpless others may come to your rescue, so why bother to be strong? When you are "sick" others may take care of you.

This fits well if a person experienced in helplessness, i.e. a "Victim", marries a "Rescuer".[5] A relationship like this is not uncommon. A "rescuer" is someone who enjoys being strong and solving other people's problems. "Rescuers" and "victims" are made for each other and can go through life feeding one another's neuroses. They meet each other's needs, but only if both continue to play the "game".

Bill and Frances were such a couple. Bill was a jovial man, for whom nothing was too much trouble.

He was a kind person, who hated conflict and settled for peace at any price. He did not feel very good about himself and covered this up by going out of his way to be nice and helpful to everybody. "No", was a word missing from his vocabulary.

Frances grew up in a home where she was expected to achieve but was never affirmed or praised. When she did not think she would be able to reach a goal, she would become sick or depressed. This would save her from the humiliation of not measuring up to her parents' or her own expectations. She found in Bill someone who did not put any demands on her and would take care of her whenever she felt she could not cope. Bill found in her someone who could always be relied on to provide some problem for him to solve!

The difficulty was that neither of them felt fulfilled in their relationship. Bill carried around a deep anger, which he found hard to acknowledge. Occasionally, he would explode and berate Frances. This made her depressed. Bill would feel very guilty and try to make amends by being especially attentive to her needs. This would continue until the next episode. Although Frances liked being rescued, she was in fact a very capable person and was frustrated by her behaviour. Both Bill and Frances found it hard to acknowledge their root problems, and each saw it as the other's fault. Eventually, they learned to take responsibility for their own feelings and behaviour, not their partner's. Frances stopped relying on Bill to make her feel better and Bill resisted the temptation to rescue Frances. As each grew in self-esteem and confidence, they were able to offer to the other true encouragement and support to help deal with his or her own issues. They learned to be real with one another and started building a satisfying relationship based on honesty and love.[6]

## Rationalisation and denial

Another way some people with low self-esteem choose to deal with their feelings is to rationalise them away. They say things like: "But everybody feels like that"; "Compared with so-and-so, I'm not too bad"; "You can't be expected to win them all"; "That's just the way I'm made"; "There's nothing you can do about it, is there?; "It's best not to think too much about it"; "I just hand it over to the Lord." These responses reflect a sense of hopelessness, or denial, or an unwillingness to get in touch with the inner pain and deal with it.

## Blaming others

There is a great temptation to blame our background, if we become aware of deficiencies in our upbringing. While there is value in identifying causes for low self-esteem, there is no value in apportioning blame. All parents make mistakes, but most parents do the best they can. Their parenting abilities depend largely on two factors: how they feel about themselves and the experiences they had in their own childhood.

Blaming someone else was the first trick in the book. When God asked Adam if he had eaten the forbidden fruit, he said: "The woman *you* put here with me – *she* gave me some fruit . . . and I ate it" (italics ours).[7] In other words, "I'm not to blame. It's Eve's fault, and in fact really your fault for creating her!" People continue to blame God, their parents, their partner, their children, their job, their looks, their lack of money or their poor education. Their purpose in blaming is not to find answers that will help them deal with the problem, but to make excuses as a way of avoiding responsibility.

## Projection

This means avoiding my own issues by pointing the finger at someone else. This is a very common pattern in some marriages that are in trouble. Partners project their faults onto the other, rather than face their own inadequacies. They try to change their partner rather than change their own attitudes and behaviour. This hurts but does not work.

A classic example of projection in Scripture is when Nathan went to talk to David about his sins of adultery and murder by proxy.[8] He told David a story about a rich man who refused to kill one of his own flock to provide a meal for a visitor, but took a poor man's only lamb for this purpose. David was so angry when he heard this, he said: "The man who did this deserves to die!" He was projecting his own guilt onto the man in the story. Then Nathan said to David, "You are the man!" That was a very courageous thing for Nathan to do, as David could have put him to death. But David's heart was smitten. He confessed his sin and dealt honestly with the issue. This is the only valid response whenever God convicts us of changes we need to make in our lives.

## Self-deception

The defence mechanisms we develop and the distorted beliefs we cling to can become a system of self-deception. This blinds us to reality, stops us from seeing ourselves objectively and blocks us from making changes. Plato said: "There is nothing worse than self-deception, where the deceiver is always with you!"[9] It often requires a strong challenge from others to find a chink in our armour. The truth of the word of God operates like this, through the working of the Holy Spirit in our minds.[10]

How can we deal with our faulty belief system and destructive patterns of behaviour that have developed? Here is a place to start:

# EXAMINE AND CHALLENGE YOUR BELIEFS ABOUT LIFE

In Chapters 2 and 3 we described the origin of our beliefs, tracing them back to childhood messages that we received from the significant people in our lives such as parents, grandparents, teachers and older siblings. These are sometimes called *"Parent messages"*. Some of the messages are true and right; others are false and destructive. Some are positive messages about ourselves, other people, the world, life and God.[11] Others are negative.

Early in life we all pick up a mixture of positive and negative messages, which we internalise without evaluating them. Child psychologists point out that children are good observers but *poor interpreters*. They are excellent mimics, but have little skill in evaluating. So these messages are just absorbed and become part of our belief system without our realising it. In turn, these attitudes to life affect our feelings and behaviour.

One of our main needs, as we grow up in a complex and unpredictable world, is for *security*; not only in an outward physical sense, but also internally. We have to make sense of what our senses tell us. The more predictable life is the more we feel in control. So, as children, we build up patterns of thinking which become habitual. These can develop into a permanent mindset which determines our attitudes and values.

These attitudes and values become our *world view*; or the philosophy by which we view ourselves and the world around us. The Roman philosopher Epictetus said, in about AD 100: "Men are disturbed not by things, but by the view they have of them."[12] Our view of the world, and particularly the view we have of ourselves in relation to the world, determines the quality of our lives. The Talmud puts it this way: "We do not see things as they are, but as we are."

Let us apply this to our decisions. Fixed attitudes become the "taped messages" in our minds. When faced with a choice about a course of action, it is as if a tape comes on in the brain: "You won't make it"; "You can do it"; "Never trust a stranger"; "Always assume the best about people"; or one of many hundreds more. Some of them are positive and some are negative. These concepts are constantly being expressed in our *internal dialogue*. This self-talk goes on all the time in our minds. This is healthy. Other people only worry about our sanity when we talk out loud, especially if we answer ourselves back!

When we say things to ourselves repeatedly, they become beliefs or convictions. In particular, we are considering here our beliefs concerning ourselves. It is the summation of these beliefs and attitudes which give us a good or bad self-concept. Some of our attitudes to ourselves are going to be faulty and distorted. Others are valid and lead to healthy

living. How are we to know the difference? We will
never know if we leave them undisturbed, if we
avoid looking at them, and if we are not prepared
to challenge them.

Figure 6 summarises the process just described:

| | |
|---|---|
| 'PARENT MESSAGES' | from significant adults in our childhood |
| ATTITUDES & VALUES | about self, others, the world, life & God |
| INTERNAL DIALOGUE | reinforced by self-talk and our 'tapes' |
| CONVICTIONS | these become our 'world view' |
| SELF-CONCEPT | defined as our attitude to ourselves |
| HEALTHY | a good self-esteem, to be re-inforced |
| UNHEALTHY | a poor self-esteem, to be changed |

**Figure 6.** Development of Our Self-Concept

Having a good look at these basic attitudes and
values, that we may have never considered before,
can be disturbing. It is not a task for the faint-
hearted! On lifting up a big rock in the garden, we

may discover a lot of creepy-crawly things underneath. In the same way, it can be scary to look inside at things we have tried to bury for so long. To maintain the philosophy of "out of sight, out of mind" often seems to be the easiest option. Unfortunately, this does not stop the damaging effects of distorted thinking on our lives and relationships. The good news is that crippling attitudes, like some garden insects, will die if exposed to the light. At least when we can see them we can do something about them.

High above the plains of Greece, on Mount Parnassus, stand the ruins of a temple that is 2,500 years old. Inscribed on a marble pillar is a two word summary of ancient Greek wisdom, which has been attributed to Socrates: "KNOW THYSELF." Knowing myself means discovering who I am inside, and bringing to the light the values and attitudes I have developed. The following process is a helpful way of doing this.

# THE EVALUATING PROCESS

There are a number of simple steps which will enable me to identify, clarify, and evaluate any view I have of myself:

1   What is it I really believe about myself in relation to this issue?
2   Where did this belief come from?
3   What is the rationale to support this belief?
4   Are there any flaws in my logic, i.e. could I be wrong?
5   Would another person come to the same conclusion about me?

6    Would I come to this conclusion about some other
     person in a similar situation to myself?
7    Is my belief consistent with the biblical view
     of me?
8    Should I stay with my original belief or do I need
     to change it?

Working through these challenging questions will
bring my belief out into the light and enable me
to test it thoroughly. Here are some brief comments
about each step.

**Step 1** Probably the hardest part of the process is
to identify your true view of yourself, especially if it
is distorted. But having identified it, you can then
strongly affirm a positive opinion of yourself, or you
can challenge the distortion and decide to change it.

**Step 2** It is helpful to find out where your beliefs
come from. Very often they start with childhood
experiences. Sometimes these will come back to
you in a flash, and you can name the person and
what was said. At other times you will need to sit
quietly and project yourself back into your childhood
memories. Picture yourself in your old home setting.
See your parents and family around you. Hear what
they are saying. Feel the feelings you had then. This
may help you to understand how a belief originated.
This is an *awareness* exercise, not an opportunity to
apportion blame, or make excuses. Identifying the
origin of a wrong belief makes it more understandable and facilitates change.

**Step 3** Young children think intuitively and not
rationally. During childhood many of your beliefs
about yourself were formed. However, as an adult

you can assess your childhood beliefs with the knowledge and experience of life which you did not have then. Does the belief that you are evaluating have a sound, reasonable basis? St Paul wrote: "When I was a child, I talked like a child, I thought like a child, I reasoned like a child. When I became a man, I put childish ways behind me."[13]

**Step 4** Sometimes we may apply "logic" to support an illogical belief, which we find hard to let go. We need to test our reasoning to discover if there are any flaws in it. The more objective opinion of another person can be a help.

**Step 5 & 6** Putting yourself in the shoes of someone else is another way to see yourself more objectively. Try it both ways: a) Would another person have the same view of yourself as you do? b) Would you be as hard on another person as you are on yourself over this issue?

**Step 7** Does the view you have of yourself, whether over-inflated or under-estimated, match up with Scripture? Is it consistent with God's view of humanity that we described in the last chapter? This is a very useful guideline. See 1 Corinthians 2:15–16.

**Step 8** If you have evaluated the old view you have of yourself and found it to be inadequate, you need to "edit" or "rewrite" a new belief, based on truth and reality. Subject this new belief to the same critical analysis that you applied to the old one.

Sharon is one person who used this evaluating process. She grew up with a picture of herself as someone who was incompetent and inferior. She doesn't remember anyone actually telling her that but she believed that this was what everyone thought about her. Her older sister was very pretty and her parents and friends often commented on her good looks. Because Sharon did not get similar comments, she concluded that she was ugly. She was an above average student, but her parents never praised her. They only encouraged her to do better. So she always thought she had failed. When someone asked Sharon to marry him, she found it hard to believe that he really loved her and was not just taking pity on her!

To develop a new picture of herself, Sharon worked through these eight steps. She was surprised to identify the source of her negative attitudes towards her looks and intelligence. She realised that there was no objective evidence to support these beliefs about herself. Sharon found it hard to know whether another person would think the same things about her or not, but was sure she would not come to these conclusions about a person like herself.

As a committed Christian, Sharon realised that God had made her a beautiful person and that she was not only loved but lovable. This enabled her to fully accept her husband's love and she started to share herself with him in a new way. She took responsibility for herself, stopped putting herself down and began to treat herself with the respect and dignity that she conferred on others.

## EDITING YOUR OLD TAPES

We all have some negative beliefs about ourselves that have built up over the years. It seems to be part of our fallen human nature to put a negative interpretation on ourselves and our experiences of life. Certainly, Satan would like us to focus on our failures and inadequacies, because then we may be overcome by discouragement and lose sight of Christ.

Dealing with our beliefs in this way is like editing the taped messages in our brains. Combining our adult maturity with a healthy understanding of God and the Scriptures, we can erase our faulty tapes and then record new ones. We then need to play the new tape frequently in our minds. New thoughts can replace old ones. This is part of the "re-parenting" process we all have to do at some time. No one can do it for you. It is done best in an attitude of prayer, seeking the Holy Spirit's guidance and understanding. A good counsellor can faciliate this process.

The following are some of the common negative tapes that play in many people's minds. These can keep us from becoming all that we are created to be. They will stop us from growing emotionally and developing a good sense of self-worth.

## SOME COMMON DISTORTED MESSAGES ABOUT OURSELVES

1 I have to please others in order to be liked or valued.
2 Expressing my wishes or desires is selfish.
3 Unless I am perfect in all I do, I am not a worthwhile person.
4 Admitting my feelings is a sign of weakness.
5 For a Christian to admit to negative feelings is a "bad witness".
6 Nobody would really want to love me for who I am, so I must earn their love.
7 I must always be busy doing something profitable to earn the right to be alive.

8  I should always put other people before myself, otherwise I will never be truly happy.

9  I am not an attractive person, so nobody would be interested in me.

10  I am not responsible for the way I am, so there is nothing I can do about it.

11  I am responsible for other people's feelings and their behaviour towards me.

12  I never trust anybody because they will always let me down.

13  It is too risky to be real and show who I am to others.

14  I must be in control of my feelings at all times, otherwise I will be too vulnerable.

15  If I reach out to others I will always be hurt, so it is safer to be a "private" person at all times.

16  To acknowledge my gifts and abilities is to be proud.

17  If I put myself down and devalue my achievements it will prove I am a humble person.

18  I must be strong at all times, otherwise life will be unmanageable.

19  It is my responsibility to keep the peace, at any price, in all my relationships.

20  I don't deserve it when things go well in my life.

21  Life is to be endured, not enjoyed. To enjoy life is sinful or at least irresponsible.

22  I will not question my beliefs, because if any of these should be proved wrong, it makes me a failure.

23  I have to be perfect, otherwise God will punish me.

24  To love myself is to be indulgent or self-centred.

25  God can't love me as I am because I am not good enough.

# DEALING WITH DISTORTED MESSAGES

Old "tapes" can be hard to erase, because they are more related to how we *feel* about ourselves than to what we consciously think. To change them usually requires a radical shift in our values and beliefs. How do we achieve this?

## Identify them

First of all, damaging messages about ourselves must be clearly identified. Once we have done this, the process of change is possible, and sometimes can happen quite quickly. We suggest that you think through the above list of distorted messages, one by one. How many of them can you recognise as your own, either in their present form, or in some variation of it? We ourselves have certainly had to challenge and re-write a number of these distorted messages over the years, and are still working on some of them.

The actual "tape" that comes on in our minds is often a shortened version of one of the above. For example, numbers 3 and 23 could be: "Be perfect!"; number 4 "Don't feel!"; number 10 "Avoid responsibility!"; number 15 "Play it safe!"

Number 7, for me (John), has been: "Don't waste time!" This message used to control my life, even though I was unaware of it. As a young man I had become totally task-oriented. This had value in terms of achieving goals and even motivating others. However, it was at the cost of neglecting my own emotional and spiritual growth. It also prevented me from putting time and energy into developing true intimacy and closeness with Agnes and our children. Changing this message has been hard to do but has turned my life around.

### Take control of them

Once damaging messages have been identified they must be challenged. They are *lies* and must be exposed to the truth. Christians have a wonderful resource to help them do this. St Paul tells us: "The weapons we fight with are not the weapons of the world. On the contrary, they have divine power to demolish strongholds. We demolish arguments and every pretension that sets itself up against the knowledge of God, and we take captive every thought to make it obedient to Christ."[14]

Negative thinking about ourselves and distorted messages that we take on board as we grow up become like "strongholds" of discouragement and fear. These "arguments" can set themselves up against the truth of our intrinsic value and worth to God and his love for us. But we are told to "take them captive" and make them "obedient to Christ". Notice that it says *we must do this*. It is a deliberate act of the will. WE must take them captive and WE are to make them obedient to Christ.

### Change them

Having identified and challenged the distorted message about yourself, you can then change it. Discovering the truth of the word of God about yourself will be of great help. Take the first statement on the list of distorted messages as an example: "I have to please others in order to be liked or valued."

This is clearly not true because it is impossible to please everybody. This does not mean we should go around deliberately upsetting people, but neither should our goal be to ingratiate ourselves with everyone. This will encourage people to despise us, not like us. St Paul told his friends in Galatia: "I am not trying to please you by sweet talk and flattery; no, I am trying to please God. If I were still trying to please men I could not be Christ's servant."[15] So a true statement to replace this distorted one would be: "*I have to be real to be liked and valued by others.*" Having changed the message, use a simple prayer like this:

Lord Jesus, I realise I have believed this lie about myself. Forgive me for this and I bring this thought under your control. Help me to discover my true identity and worth in you.

AMEN

## Reinforce the new messages

Old messages have taken many years to develop their grip on us. The old "tapes" have become familar paths in our brains by virtue of the many times we have used them. When we changed the "tape", the decision may have been real and we truly believed the new message. However, the new path is not very distinct yet. When faced with a choice again, whether to follow the old track or the new, the familiar one is so obvious and the new one rather indistinct. The only way to strengthen the new path is to reinforce it, in the same way as walking across a new path on a grassy hillside establishes the new track. By the same token, every time we choose the new path instead of the old, the original one starts to become less obvious until it is eventually lost.

There are many ways in which we can reinforce

new messages in our brains, *provided they are true and we really believe them*. We can repeat the new truth to ourselves, silently or out loud, on a daily basis. We can share it with a close friend or partner who can reaffirm its truth to us. Another way is to write it out and fix it to the bathroom mirror or on the door of the refrigerator as a daily reminder. Record it in your journal where you can return to it frequently, or write it on a bookmarker. Keep reinforcing it in your mind in as many ways as you can in order to counteract the many times the old message has controlled your life. Thomas à Kempis wrote, "Habit overcomes habit."[16]

Here is how one couple worked on distorted messages that had spoiled their relationship. Jim grew up in a home where he formed the impression that he was not good enough. It seemed to him that he was never able to fulfil his parents' expectations, or to please them. His father was very disappointed that his only son was not good at sport or interested in cars. Jim was quite academic, but he received no affirmation or encouragement in his studies from his parents while he was at school or university.

So Jim withdrew into himself. He became a remote person, who never shared his feelings with others, even his family. His wife, Sally, felt shut out of his life. At first she blamed herself. For a while she "battered on Jim's door to get in". But for the last few years she had given up. To admit his feelings, especially anger or incompetence, was evidence of weakness to Jim. He had to give the appearance of being in control at all times. Life certainly was not something to be enjoyed. Jim had never felt loved as a child and could not believe that anyone, even Sally, would want to love him.

As time went by, Jim became very defensive,

withdrawn and even depressed at times. Sally felt increasingly lonely in their unrewarding relationship. She felt very guilty about this, because she realised this kind of marriage was not what God wanted for them. To compensate, she put all her energy into the children and church-related activities. Jim interpreted this as yet another rejection, which reinforced his childhood "tape" that he was "not good enough".

Fortunately, Jim and Sally both wanted to do something about their marriage. Jim began to examine the beliefs he had about himself and to understand their source. He challenged the deeply ingrained message that he was "not good enough", and realised that there was no rational basis for this belief. He struggled with this and is still working on it. But he began to discover his worth and value to God and to appreciate the talents and abilities he had been given. Jim and Sally learned the skills of being able to share their feelings with each other. This enabled them to open up and be real with one another. They also learned how to "encourage one another and build each other up"[17] and reaffirm each other's self-worth frequently.

## SUMMARY

Taking responsibility for our self-esteem is the basic step in the process of change and growth in this area. A healthy self-image is a choice. We also need help from God and often from other people, but they cannot take the initial step for us. Faulty beliefs and distorted messages that we picked up in childhood can be changed.

# REFLECTIONS AND EXERCISES

1 How much do you take responsibility for what happens in your life?

- Make a list in your journal of things for which you assume responsibility and another list of situations where you are aware of avoiding responsibility.
- Think back over the past few weeks to any situations where you have avoided responsibility by blaming someone or something else for what may have gone wrong. How could you have acted differently?

2 "When you think back over your life, do you feel like an observer who is reading the story, or do you feel like the author writing the story?"[18] Discuss this question in your group.

3 On a scale of 1–10 estimate your level of self-esteem:

1–3  Dissatisfied with your self-image and how you feel about yourself. You realise that you have a low self-esteem.

4–7  Aware of problems in this area.

8–10 Comfortable with yourself and reasonably satisfied with your self-esteem (but still with room for growth).

- The results of the Self-Esteem Evaluation Test (Chapter 2, exercise 10) will help you make a reasonably accurate assessment here.
- Ask two or three people who know you well and whom you can trust, to do this assessment of you as well.

Clearly, this is not a precise measurement but it will give you an indication of whether you need to work on this issue. Record your thoughts and the opinion of your friends in your journal.

4 What is your level of motivation for making changes and working towards growth in your self-esteem:
LOW...................MEDIUM...................HIGH?

- If your motivation is low or medium, re-read the section in this chapter headed: "Things That Prevent Us Making Changes". For example:

  Are you afraid of change for some reason?
  Can you see evidence of "learned helplessness" in your behaviour?
  What degree of denial is operating in your thinking?
  Do you blame others or circumstances for your present situation?
  Are you projecting your problem onto others?

These are searching questions to ask yourself. The best way to do this exercise is in a group setting or with the support of a friend, where you can get feedback and help each other.

5 Write down as many beliefs about yourself that you can think of:

e.g. "I am a competent person."
"I usually make mistakes and get things wrong."
"Other people matter more than I do."
"I only feel good about myself when doing something useful."

- Reading through the twenty-five distorted messages listed in this chapter may help you identify some of your own distortions.
- Recalling some of your *family mottos* is also helpful:

  e.g. "Work before pleasure."
       "Never share any family secrets or problems with others."
       "FHB." ("Family hold back.")
       "When the going gets tough, the tough get going."

  This is a good way to discover "Parent messages", which can be the origin of certain "tapes" that we take with us into life.

- Take each of these beliefs about yourself in turn and submit it to the Evaluating Process described in this chapter. Do this exercise on your own first. It can be helpful to work through them with a close friend or in a supportive group. Deal with each one systematically:

**Old "tape"**   Write down the belief you have identified.

**Source**       Try to identify where this belief comes from in your past. Quite frequently, beliefs that we accept as adults have a deeper root in childhood experiences.

**Logic**        Write down as clearly as you can the rationale behind this belief. Is it consistent with your experience of life and your understanding of God and Scripture?

**Error**        If you are unable to substantiate

|             |                                      |
| ----------- | ------------------------------------ |
|             | this belief, identify what you think is the error. |
| New "tape"  | Write out a new statement of belief about yourself, i.e. a new "tape" to replace the old one. |
| Prayer      | Bring your "old tape" captive to Christ and ask him to help you establish the new and true one. |
| Action      | Write the new belief on a card. Keep it with you and refer to it often. Fix another to the bathroom mirror or the door of the refrigerator so you will see it frequently. Own it as yours. |

6 In a well known book, *Your Child's Self Esteem*[19] the author lists eight factors that prevent low self-esteem, as follows:
1) An accepting family.
2) A teacher who respects your person.
3) A job that particularly fits your talents.
4) A warm confirming friend or marriage partner.
5) A meaningful religious philosophy.
6) An introspective and challenging attitude towards your basic assumptions.
7) Meaningful reading.
8) Individual or group therapy.

Most of these factors have been referred to throughout this book.

- Reflect on each of these eight elements in terms of your background and experience, recording your thoughts in your journal.

  Perhaps some have been more significant than others.

Maybe you missed out on one or more of these experiences in your childhood.
Are there any of them that you could do something about now?

• Share what you want to in your small group.

# SEVEN

# UNDERSTANDING YOURSELF

*The unexamined life is not worth living*

Sophocles, 496–406 BC

In Chapter 5 we looked at how God sees us and the difference it makes when we see things from God's perspective. Then we thought of Socrates' words: "Know thyself", as being the starting point from which we can make changes. To know yourself is rewarding, but it can also be a little frightening. Goethe wrote: "Know thyself? If I knew myself, I'd run away!" Many people feel like running away when they have a look inside, especially when using the searchlight of God's word. In this section we want to focus on a process of self-discovery.

When Sophocles said: "The unexamined life is not worth living" he was expressing a need that we all have to discover who we are and how we function. This is not unhealthy introspection or narcissism.[1] For a visual person (someone whose primary way of receiving information is visually), examining yourself means to have an honest *look* at who you are. If you happen to be primarily an auditory person, stop and *listen* to yourself. And if you are a kinesthetic person (someone whose primary communication mode is via touch or feelings), how does it *feel* to be you? In fact, we really need to do all three: look, listen and feel. "Listening to our true self is a way of really loving ourselves and it makes it possible for others to love us as well."[2]

What we are talking about here is *self-examination* but not self-pre-occupation. This is something the Old Testament writers were not afraid to do, and they sought God's help in the task. David asked God: "Test me, O Lord, and try me, examine my heart and my mind."[3] "Search me, O God, and know my heart; test me and know my anxious thoughts. See if there is any offensive way in me, and lead me in the way everlasting."[4] Clearly, this process was not for God's benefit, but for David's. God already knew what was in David's mind and heart, but David did not. So he asked God to help him discover what was hidden there. Solomon wondered: "How then can anyone understand his own way?", then answers his own question: "The lamp of the Lord searches the spirit of a man; it searches out his inmost being."[5]

This process of knowing ourselves is an essential part of our spiritual and personal growth. St Augustine prayed: "I beseech you God to show my full self to myself."[6] Richard Foster puts it: "Through faith, self knowledge leads us to self acceptance and a self love that draw their life from God's acceptance and love."[7] We will explore this process in the next chapter. But as we start to examine ourselves, we discover that we are essentially two people:

I. **THE PERSON**      This is my real self; my inner self, my feelings; the self of reality, the self of experience.

II. **THE PERSONAGE**  Refers to my self-picture, the image I have of myself; my ideal self; often the mask I wear.

Dr Paul Tournier explores this concept in his book *The Meaning of Persons*.[8] He wrote it in French and the original title of his book is "Le Personnage et la Personne". The personage is how we present ourselves to the world: our image or mask. Carl Jung used the word "persona", (which is Latin for "mask", especially one worn by an actor) to refer to the personage. In classical times, actors in a play wore masks to complement their voices. They were portraying something that was different from themselves.

Like an actor, I will often present to others a personage which is different from my person, although sometimes it is difficult to distinguish between the two. It is even possible to have a genuine belief that the image I have of myself is the real me. It is similar to watching a good play. Sometimes the acting is so realistic we forget the players are acting parts designed by another. Tournier states: "The person and the personage are linked, yet remain distinct. I can approach the person only through that image, which at one and the same time allows me glimpses of it and also tends to hide it from me; reveals as well as conceals it."[9]

The further these two selves are apart, the more *internal conflict and tension* there will be. This is one of the major causes of stress and tension in a person's life. The conflict is between the self of reality and the self-picture; the inner self and the image that is presented to the world. Within a blustering man, who seems to be in control, there is often a frightened little boy. An insecure girl may be concealed within a composed performer on the stage of life.

Conversely, the more integrated my person and

my personage are, the less internal tension I will experience. The more at peace I am within myself the stronger will be my self-esteem. But if I am uncomfortable with what I know is within me and unsure of my worth and value, I will be tempted to live mostly in the unreal world of my self-picture. This may bring a temporary truce in the "civil war" within, but at the cost of inhibiting emotional and spiritual growth.

How I see myself determines how I *project myself* to others. This is the main determinant of the quality of my relationships. If I am living more in the inner self of reality, in touch with my feelings and open to truth, I will come across as genuine, authentic and real. But if I am constantly hiding behind my personage or my self-picture, it will be apparent to others that I am living a role or wearing a mask.

Most of us can identify a conflict between roles and reality in our lives. For example, I (John) am aware that I am basically a tender-hearted person. However, as I was growing up, I picked up the message at school that real boys were not like that; they were tough and "cool". So I tried to repress any tender feelings. One of my strongest "tapes" was, "Big boys don't cry". Later on, as a medical student, I was confronted with many tragic situations and found it easier to repress my real feelings about people and concentrate on their immediate medical needs. But I am so glad I discovered that my "personage" was wrong; that it is healthy for men to show their tenderness and to express these feelings appropriately. I also received "permission" to cry at times, for my own needs, as well as when others were in distress.[10]

Professional life can provide protection, too. I

(Agnes) really enjoyed my nursing career, with its many opportunities to help people in need. But sometimes there were situations where I did not feel very confident. On looking back, I realise how much I relied on my nurse's uniform and mask to cover up psychologically as well as physically. I felt protected, and used the uniform to project someone who was not really me. That was uncomfortable for me as a person, until I learned to be more confident and real in my role as a nurse. Figure 7 summarises what we have been saying:

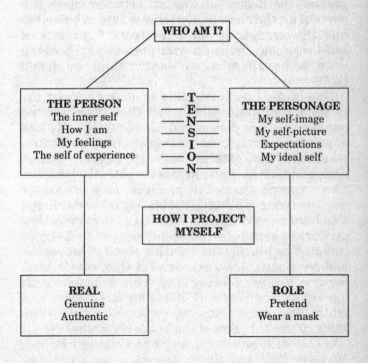

**Figure 7.** The Person and the Personage

Of course, we have *many appropriate roles in life*.[11] A man can wear a number of "hats", for example: husband, father, accountant, church elder, chairman of a committee, member of a club, etc. A woman may be a wife, mother, school teacher, home group leader and so forth. Each role is different and has different expectations in terms of behaviour. But truly integrated people are *able to be real in all of these roles* and not put on "masks" in order to impress others. They have closed the "credibility gap" between their person and their personage. The greater the degree of overlap between these two parts of us, the more comfortable we are in ourselves and the stronger is our self-esteem. "Our lack of self-love comes from an ever-present gap between what we are and what we want or think we should be."[12]

One of the things which is so striking about the biography of Jesus is the fact that there was no gap between his person and his personage. He had a number of roles, for example: child, carpenter, teacher, healer, prophet, Messiah, Saviour. But in each of these he came across as patently genuine. There was no attempt at pretence, no posturing or mask-wearing. The religious leaders of the day found this hard to cope with. It was this authenticity that produced a sense of wonder and awe as the disciples reflected on his life: the amazing blend of his person and personage. John expressed it this way: "Christ became a human being and lived here on earth among us and was full of loving forgiveness and truth. And some of us have seen his glory – the glory of the only Son of the heavenly Father."[13]

In her delightful allegory, *The Velveteen Rabbit*, Margery Williams illustrates the beauty of being real:

"What is REAL?" asked the Rabbit one day, when they were lying side by side near the nursery fender, before Nana came to tidy the room. "Does it mean having things that buzz inside you and a stick-out handle?"

"Real isn't how you are made," said the Skin Horse. "It's a thing that happens to you. When a child loves you for a long, long time, not just to play with, but really loves you, then you become Real."

"Does it hurt?" asked the Rabbit.

"Sometimes," said the Skin Horse, for he was always truthful. "When you are Real you don't mind being hurt."

"Does it happen all at once, like being wound up," he asked, "or bit by bit?"

"It doesn't happen all at once," said the Skin Horse. "You become. It takes a long time. That's why it doesn't happen to people who break easily, or have sharp edges, or who have to be carefully kept. Generally, by the time you are Real, most of your hair has been loved off, and your eyes drop out and you get loose in the joints and very shabby. But these things don't matter at all, because once you are Real you can't be ugly, except to people who don't understand."[14]

Becoming "real" certainly does not happen quickly. Dramatic events, such as a spiritual conversion or even a painful experience can be the start. But becoming authentic and genuine is not instantaneous. As we mature, things which can hinder the process need to be overcome.

# BLOCKS TO BECOMING REAL

## Fear

People fear many things in the world around them, but the biggest battle with fear is usually fought within. We can be afraid to look inwards and face what is there. We may be aware of things that we do not like about ourselves, but are afraid to change. If I am afraid to examine my heart and discover what may need to change, I certainly will not want others to know about it. So this results in a fear of intimacy and a reluctance to allow anyone to come too close.

## Judgemental attitudes

One of the things which prevents us from truly being ourselves is our tendency to judge ourselves harshly. Many people judge themselves even more critically than they would judge others. Persistent self-criticism is demeaning and undermines self-esteem.

Jesus said: "Do not judge, or you too will be judged."[15] This is because our assessment of people is flawed by our inadequate knowledge of them. We do not know their motives or their hearts as God does. But this command can be *applied equally to ourselves*. Do not judge yourself summarily either, because you do not see the full picture of yourself either, as God can.[16]

Jesus does not pass this kind of judgement on people. The classic example of this is recorded in John chapter 8. The Pharisees brought to him a woman caught in the act of adultery, whom they had judged already and were about to stone to death. Jesus said to them: "You judge by human standards; I pass judgment on no one" (v 15). But to the woman he said: "Neither do I condemn you, go now and leave your life of sin" (v 11). While he did not condemn her as a person, he judged what she had done. In the same way, we too must make judgements on issues, i.e. what is right and wrong,[17] but we are not to judge people, including ourselves.

Jenny was a person who was hypercritical of herself. If she forgot a friend's birthday she accused herself of being self-centred and thoughtless. When she had been sharp with a customer at work, she would agonise at night about being such a rude person. It took some time to help her see that the reason for her forgetfulness was not so much selfishness as trying to fit too many things into her life, and that consequently she had little time to plan what she wanted to do. Also, her occasional negative reaction to a customer arose not from a deliberate desire to be rude but from her insecurity in the job. She came to understand that her overly critical attitude to herself actually blocked her from making changes. This freed her to live consistently with her high standards without being inhibited by them.

## Inadequate self-evaluation

Another thing which prevents us from being real is failure to assess ourselves properly, either by putting ourselves down or else over-estimating ourselves. While this may not harm us as much as devastating criticism can, it still leaves us in an unreal world and unable to grow towards maturity.

St Paul tells us to guard against both extremes: "For by the grace given me I say to every one of you: Do not think of yourself more highly than you ought, but rather think of yourself with sober judgement, in accordance with the measure of faith

God has given you."[18] The Living Bible reads: "Be honest in your estimate of yourselves." According to Paul, the process of self assessment which we are talking about in this chapter is a valid one, and Christians have been given faith to help them do it realistically.

This discipline of self-analysis needs to be kept in balance with other mental capacities which can help us remain open to change and growth. One valuable ability is our imagination.

# THE POWER OF IMAGINATION

The honest evaluating of ourselves, that we have been describing, is a *left-brain activity*. Left brain functions include rational, analytical, logical, critical thinking. These are fine in their place, and we need to use these faculties. But we also need the balance of *right-brain functions*, which include imaginative, symbolic, creative and intuitive activities. One of the most powerful is the gift of imagination, which Albert Einstein claimed was more important than knowledge. Creative imagination, or the use of a mental picture, tempered with realism, can give us the vision to make significant changes in our lives.

We do not need to fear using our imagination, although like any gift, it can be misused. For example, there is a popular theory which goes something like this: "You can be what you want to be. Just imagine hard enough that you are successful and rich and it will happen!" Also, our imagination can become out of control and lead us into sin.

The Hebrew word for imagination is "yetser", and is translated in the Old Testament (in the AV) as "imagination" five times, and once as "mind". Our imagination can be a *force both for evil or for good*. God sent the flood because "the wickedness of man was great in the earth, and that every imagination of the thoughts of his heart was only evil continually".[19] King David was aware of this danger and so prayed that God would keep the imaginations of the people of Israel, especially of his son Solomon, loyal to the Lord.[20] Isaiah writes: "You will keep in perfect peace him whose mind [*yetser*] is steadfast, because he trusts in you."[21] So our imagination can become a stabilising force and *source of peace* in our lives if it is directed properly.

All of us use our imagination constantly, sometimes positively and sometimes negatively. Every time we think about a future event, we have a picture in our minds about what it will be like. This is part of being human. People with low self-esteem usually imagine the worst about themselves and presume others are thinking poorly of them. They think negatively about the future most of the time and cannot imagine that life could be any different. On the other hand, healthy use of our imagination, balanced by reality and faith, can help us move towards more positive goals.

The great Methodist preacher, Dr Leslie D. Weatherhead wrote:

> If we have in our minds a picture of ourselves as fear-haunted and defeated nobodies, we must get rid of that picture and hold up our heads. That is a false picture and the false must go. God sees us as men and women in whom and through whom he can do a great work. He sees us as already serene, confident and cheerful. He sees us, not as pathetic victims of life, but masters of the art of living; not wanting

sympathy, but imparting help to others, and therefore thinking less and less of ourselves; and full, not of self-concern but of love and laughter and a desire to serve.[22]

*Picturing*

If you can see yourself as you could be, in a realistic way, it will certainly help you to become that person. Athletes enter a race with a picture of themselves winning, or at least doing well.[23] If not, they are bound to fail. In the same way, successful actors and entertainers first see in their minds the way in which they wish to perform. If you see yourself becoming the open, confident, growing person that God designed you to be, that is how you will begin to live. For the Christian, the Holy Spirit's strength is available to help you work towards your goal.

George used his God-given ability to form pictures in his mind. His father had walked out on the family when he was only five, and his mother was a rather unstable person. He grew up feeling very insecure, and longed for the stability of a loving father. When he became a Christian, he used to picture his relationship with Father God, based on what he knew about God from the Scriptures. As a sheep farmer, he found it easy to see the Lord as his Shepherd,[24] hear him calling him by name[25] and leading him through rough places to pasture and water. Dwelling on this metaphor in his imagination helped him develop a strong relationship with God and gave him a sense of confidence. He was using his imagination to strengthen his relationship with the Good Shepherd.

Jesus used people's ability to see pictures in their minds as his main form of communication. He taught profound truths in simple word-pictures, or parables, because the people found it hard to understand in any other way.[26] But there was another reason. He knew that ideas communicated in a picture form are more likely to remain in the mind and heart and so bear fruit. For example, he called the word of God "the seed" and our hearts "the soil"; he is "the vine" and we are "the branches"; he is "the shepherd" and we are "the sheep". The New Testament, writers used scores of word-pictures, for example, the Christian life is like running a race; the Church is a body made up of many parts or a building with many stones.

## Practising

Once having seen and clearly identified your desired behaviour, you can practise it in your head. Concert pianists often practise playing the music in their heads. Orators and preachers constantly turn over what they are going to say in their minds and rehearse the right turn of phrase. Successful salesmen do the same. Before approaching a potential buyer, they postulate difficult selling scenarios and think of a successful pitch for each.

The same principle applies to life in terms of the kind of person I want to be. If I believe I should be a more loving person, I can imagine difficult situations with a particular person whom I find hard to love and practise in my mind a kindly response. If my desire is to be more Christ-like, I think of what I know of him from the Scriptures and mentally practise behaviour that is consistent with his life-style. If I want to be a more open person, I turn over in my mind ways of being more real in my encounters with people. I picture ways of being more assertive, more honest

or more genuine and practise these in my mind. I
can then ask the Lord to confirm the desire of my
heart.

## SUMMARY

Before I can grow as a person I need to understand
myself. The process of examining my life is an essential part of changing from an inadequate self-image
to a healthy self-esteem. Growth towards becoming
a whole person involves identifying my "person" and
my "personage" and blending the two. My goal is to
be real and authentic. To do this, I can combine the
cognitive process of self-evaluation with the use of
imagination.

# REFLECTIONS AND EXERCISES

1 Reflect on your "person" and your "personage".

- Head up two opposite pages in your journal: "My Person" and "My Personage". Then compare and contrast aspects of your life and behaviour in terms of what you are really like and how you see yourself; what is going on inside you and the image you present to others. Some of the paired statements will be congruent but others will be inconsistent. For example:

| MY PERSON | MY PERSONAGE |
|---|---|
| I feel unsure of my ability as a teacher. | I present myself as efficient, cool and competent. |
| I am frustrated by (.....'s) behaviour. | I put on a nice smile, bite my tongue and hide my feelings. |
| I am aware of my skills as a mediator. | I do not hesitate to assist in a dispute when asked. |
| I don't agree with the decision my partner has made. | I go along with it, without saying anything to him/her. |
| I am really sad about what (.....) is doing. | I show no evidence of my feelings, because .... |
| I admire the way my partner relates to the children. | I tell her when she has done a good job. |

NOTE: Do not worry if you can only think of a few personal examples initially but leave space to add others as they come to mind.

- If there is a discrepancy between the paired statements, try to determine the reason. Why are you afraid to be real? What would happen if you were honest? How could you be both honest about yourself and kind to others?[27]
- What effect would it have on your self-concept if any two statements that are not in agreement were to match up? What changes could

you make to reconcile your person and your personage?

- What effect would it have on your relationships if you were more authentic in the example that you are thinking about?

2 How critical are you of yourself? How many times have you judged yourself harshly this week? Are there times when you overestimate your abilities? Perhaps there have been times when you have needed to make an honest inventory of your life, but have been too scared to do so.[28] Recall such a time.

3 Spend some time reflecting on Romans 12:3 in the light of what you think about yourself. Ask God for the faith to be able to make a "sober judgement" of yourself.

4 Here are some simple exercises using imagination and picturing.

- Find a quiet place where you will not be disturbed. Spend a few moments relaxing. Take some deep breaths. Thank the Lord for his presence and ask him to make you more aware of him. Then read the passages suggested and see yourself in these situations.

    Do this on your own first, then share your experiences with your group, partner or friend.

a) *Read Luke 24:13–35*
Imagine that you are the unnamed disciple walking to Emmaus with Cleopas. (We are not told whether it was a man or a woman. It possibly was

Cleopas' wife as "they" invited Jesus to "stay with us" – v 29.) See the setting in detail: the hot dusty road; the late afternoon sun shining in your face; the feelings of sadness and desolation at Jesus' unexpected death; the stranger joining you, who is such a perfect listener (vv 17–19); the questions you would like to ask him and the replies he might make (vv 27, 32).

Imagine sharing your present problems, discouragements, struggles and fears with Jesus. What would he say to you? What might cause your "heart to burn within you"? (v 32). How might you respond, and what action could you take as a result of spending this time with Jesus? (v 33). How do you feel about the way Jesus loves you; wants to share life's journey with you; listens to you? What does this do for your sense of self-worth? Write down in your journal significant learnings or insights from this experience.

b) *Read Luke 10:38–41*
Imagine that you are either Martha, Mary or Lazarus entertaining Jesus in your home. Picture the scene with Jesus and his disciples filling the house; your responsibilities as hostess or host; the conflict between wanting to be part of the conversation and feeling responsible for your guests.

Listen to Jesus' gentle rebuke of Martha (vv 41–42). How does this speak into your life right now in terms of your goals and priorities? How does it make you feel to know that Jesus wants to be an intimate part of your life and home too? When was the last time you "ate together" with him? See Revelation 3:20.

• Record your reactions in your journal.

c) *Choose other passages or stories* from Scripture and in a similar way see yourself as part of the scene.[29] Open up your mind to whatever the Lord wants to say to you. Record insights in your journal and share what you are comfortable with in your group.

5 List in your journal a number of tasks or commitments you have ahead of you in the next few weeks. Draw up four columns in a double page of the journal, and head them:

| Event. | Positive outcome. | Negative outcome. | Result. |
| --- | --- | --- | --- |
|  |  |  |  |

- For each event visualise possible positive and negative outcomes and write down clearly what these might be.
- Focus on the positive outcomes only. See yourself achieving the goal or successfully dealing with the problem. Do this each day until the event. As you pray about them, thank the Lord for the way he is going to help you in the task. Finally, record the result after each event has taken place.
- After each event, whether you have achieved the desired outcome or not, reflect on the effect of seeing a positive outcome. What effect did it have on you as a person, in terms of how you feel about yourself? Compare this with other recent experiences where you have not used this approach. Discuss your experiment with your small group.

6 Sit upright in a chair, with your eyes closed. Imagine there is a chair in front of you, and see a person sitting in it whom you love very much. Take time to see him/her very clearly: their clothes, facial expression and posture. Tell that person how much you value him; what qualities you really like about her; and that you really love him/her. Conclude with an embrace or a kiss, or in whatever way seems appropriate. Watch as he or she walks out of the room.

• Now see yourself sitting in that chair and take time to picture yourself clearly. Then tell yourself what you like about you and the qualities you really appreciate about you. Say to yourself: "I really love you." Conclude with an appropriate farewell, and watch as you walk from the room.[30]

• Reflect on what you have experienced. Was there any significant difference between the way you related to your friend and to yourself? If so, what could be the reason? What does this exercise say about the degree to which you have learned to "love your neighbour as yourself"?

• Record any insights in your journal and discuss this experiment with your small group.

7 *A personal collage.* This is a fun exercise, best done with your group or perhaps with your family. You will need the following *materials*: several old picture magazines; coloured pens or pencils; scissors; glue; sheets of paper or card approximately 40 cm square. Share the resources in the group.

Make a collage by pasting words, symbols or pictures cut out of the magazines which represent you. Choose ones which focus on the things you like about yourself, your interests and goals. Draw in symbols, words or pictures if needed. Take your time, allowing up to an hour for this process.

Take it in turns to describe your finished collage to the group. The task of the group is to listen, perhaps ask clarifying questions, but NOT to analyse what the speaker is saying.

## EIGHT

## ACCEPT AND LOVE YOURSELF

*Love your neighbour as you love yourself.*[1]

Jesus

Taking responsibility for yourself is the beginning of a journey towards growth and change. But we cannot change what we do not understand. In the last chapter we saw that a self-examination process is essential in order to understand ourselves better. In this way we will become real, which benefits us and also our relationships. Once I understand who I am, then I can learn to accept and love myself, and I will also be able reveal myself authentically to another.

## ACCEPTANCE

Acceptance is powerful "medicine". When I experience acceptance from another human being, just as I am and without any requirement to prove my worth, I begin to feel healthy and lovable. In the climate of acceptance I can grow as a person and reach my potential. When I am truly accepted by others I can more readily accept myself. When I accept myself, I can more readily accept others. Many people have never experienced real acceptance in childhood or even in their adult relationships.

Self-acceptance sets me free from being stuck in a performance cycle, trying to prove to the world, and especially to myself, that I am a person of value. I can now strive for excellence for the sake of doing a good job, rather than having to demonstrate to myself, to my parents (whether they are alive or dead), to anyone else or even to God, that I am a worthwhile person.

Compassion and acceptance are related qualities. One leads to the other. Many people acknowledge the importance of being compassionate towards others, as Jesus was, but find it hard to be compassionate to themselves. True compassion involves accepting yourself and others. As I come to accept myself I can grow in self-esteem and learn to love myself. This also enables me to reach out in love to others and to love God more. Joyce Huggett puts it: "The prerequisite of such love is self-acceptance. We have to learn to accept ourselves in the same way as Jesus accepted himself, acknowledging both personal strengths and personal limitations. Until we do this we have only a weak, watered-down love to offer to others."[2]

Ultimately we find our true basis for self-worth in the acceptance that God offers us. Discovering this helps us to accept ourselves and then go beyond ourselves to accept others. "Accept one another, then, just as Christ accepted you",[3] was Paul's message to a congregation made up of many cultures and backgrounds. The good news is that God has accepted us in Christ.[4]

Josh McDowell describes the "Circle of Acceptance"[5] in the following diagram:

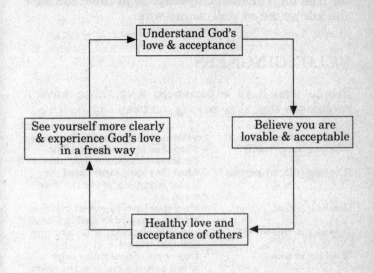

**Figure 8.** The Circle of Acceptance

To experience acceptance from people and know that they believe in us also helps us to accept and believe in ourselves. From personal experience, I (John) owe a large measure of my sense of self-worth to the fact that two women accepted me and believed in me. The first was my mother who, despite being aware of my failings, totally believed in me. On leaving school and starting medical training I was certainly not an "A-grade" student and consequently had to work very hard to keep up. One of the things that kept me going was the knowledge that my mother believed implicitly that I would make it. For her, it was not a case of "if" I graduated, but "when"! The other woman who has totally believed in me for the past forty years (to my surprise at times, because she knows me so well) is my wife.

# BELONGINGNESS

People who have experienced acceptance have a confidence that they belong, and can say:

| | |
|---|---|
| "I belong to me." | – when they fully accept themselves. |
| "I belong in my family." | – when they have experienced unconditional acceptance from parents |
| "I belong with my partner." | – when they have experienced the loving acceptance of the one they married. |
| "I belong to God." | – when they have discovered that they are fully accepted by God in Christ. |
| "I belong in this world." | – when they feel part of the universe that God created. |
| "I belong in society." | – Experience of acceptance helps us to feel part of a group, a profession, a club, a city, a nation. |

The experience of belongingness leads to a sense of identity and helps to produce a feeling of significance and worth. "Belongingness is essential . . . it positions a person with respect to other people. Belongingness gives an orientation in society as 'one of them' . . . an underlying feeling of being 'in' or 'out' with people."[6]

Many people today struggle with rootlessness – not knowing their identity. An awareness of one's pedigree, or roots, enhances a sense of self-worth. It is well known that people who emigrate to establish a home in another country often place much more importance on their cultural roots and heritage than those who never leave their native land. This helps them to preserve their identity and self-esteem while adjusting to the new environment.

We worked for a number of years in Port Moresby, the capital of Papua New Guinea. Most expatriates in the town had not immigrated into the country but were there temporarily for work purposes. We observed that many of them behaved as if they were in no-man's-land. It was as if they had lost their roots. They did not belong in that country, nor were they in their own culture. As a consequence, standards of morality and behaviour were lowered considerably. It has been observed that situations where there is a marked sense of rootlessness, such as California, often provide an environment that encourages the development of bizarre religious cults and extremes of lifestyle.[7]

Belongingness has been a very different experience for the two of us. Agnes grew up in a rural setting, within the security of a large extended family. She knew where she belonged and felt secure in a family who had lived in the same house and farm for three generations. John was born in Beijing, of parents who came from England. He had his primary schooling in China, secondary education in New Zealand and tertiary training in London. He feels more of a "child of the universe" than a citizen of any one place.

But both of us have a strong awareness of belonging to God, which gives us a deep sense of security and worth. Knowing God and being able to say, "Father, I belong to you", does so much for a person:

It gives me *roots*. "Lord, you are my origin, my Creator and I have been created in your image."
It gives me *confidence*. I know who I am, where I come from, where I belong and where I am going.

It gives me *significance*. If I belong to you, I must be of value and worth!

It gives me *security*. I feel safe. You will never leave me or let me go.[8]

It presupposes a *relationship*, one which is different from any other. I can belong WITH another human being, but can only belong TO God.[9]

It gives me a *future*. I belong to God for eternity, and nothing can separate us.[10]

# BEFRIEND YOUR BODY

In Chapter 5 we thought about the wonder of the human body. To marvel at God's incredible creation of complex human beings is a good start to self-acceptance. The psalmists expressed these thoughts frequently in their worship of God.[11]

But there may be some things about your body that you don't like. You may think that you are too short or too tall; you don't like your eye colouring, your hair, the shape of your nose, ears, or hips, etc. Surveys have shown that up to 90 per cent of people are dissatisfied with their body image.

Part of a healthy self-image is accepting yourself the way God made you. When you accept yourself physically your self-esteem improves. But excessive preoccupation with our physical features and wishing they were different is counter-productive and wastes so much time and energy. Acceptance of ourselves includes much more than accepting our physical appearance, but it usually starts there.

This moving little story illustrates the power of being accepted by another person and how this can help us to accept ourselves.

## *Do you have legs like mine?*

When I first started school, everyone made fun of my fat legs. They would call me "tree stump". Children can be so cruel. I would cry myself to sleep. As I grew older I laughed with them to cover up. No one would want to go out with me.

When I was new at college I met Mark. I liked him from the start and felt really comfortable with him. Then he asked me out and I couldn't believe it. He never made one single reference to my legs. But I did, you know, looking for assurance.

One night he took my hand and said, "I want you to stop knocking yourself. God gave you good sturdy legs. They give me a solid feeling, and I like it." I could only cry.

One week he took me home and when I met his mother I wanted to cry again . . . She'd had polio. She wore a shoe that was built up and she walked with a limp.

I looked at him, and he looked at me, and I think I loved him right then like nobody ever loved a guy before.

Author unknown[12]

Many people see their body as an enemy which produces aches and pains and will let them down. Even St Francis called his body "Brother ass". Your body is your best friend! It is "on your side". The body sends us important messages all the time, which many people try to ignore. When they get frequent headaches, migraines, excema, stomach pains or one of the other messages the body sends, they rush for some pill to take the discomfort away.

At times, medication is appropriate, but certainly not before asking: "What is the meaning behind this message?" These symptoms are usually the body's warning signals to say we are over-doing it or have unresolved issues in our lives. Never waste a good symptom! The body is your friend, so make friends with your body.

This message is not new. In about 400 BC, Hippocrates, the father of modern medicine said: "Your body is the best physician you will ever find." So we need to respect our bodies and learn to listen to them. In fact, the tongue is the only part of the body which knows how to lie.[13] The rest of the body tells the truth! Our bodies deserve respect, acceptance and our friendship.

Not only does the body send us important messages, but God may use it to speak to us. Sometimes it is the only way he can attract our attention. A regular bodily symptom is one way God lets us know that something is out of balance in our lives or that we are neglecting something important. C.S. Lewis made this observation: "God whispers to us in our joys, but shouts at us in our pains."

But we need to go further than just accepting our bodies, we must *accept the whole of who we are*, our weaknesses and our strengths, our limitations and abilities.

## STRENGTHS AND WEAKNESSES

In the last chapter we referred to St Paul's statement: "Do not think of yourself more highly than you ought, but rather think of yourself with sober judgment, in accordance with the measure of faith God has given you."[14]

This is an important principle when learning
to accept ourselves. Paul is telling us neither to
have inflated ideas of our good qualities nor to
underestimate the gifts God has given us and the
qualities we have developed by his grace. It is very
helpful to assess realistically our strengths and our
weaknesses from time to time.

There are at least three beneficial purposes of our
weaknesses or inabilities:

1) They can keep us away from being involved in
the wrong ministries and thereby save us time
and energy.
2) They allow God's power to work through us
so that we might have daily evidence of his
presence with us.
3) They can keep us interdependent with others
within the church, giving us more complete
lives.[15]

Paul said that God had taught him the principle, "My
power is made perfect in weakness". He delighted in
his weaknesses for the right reasons, and discovered
that "when I am weak, then I am strong!"[16]

It helps to reframe the term weakness and call it
a *growing area*. There is no way we can grow in these
areas until we have identified them and owned them.
Knowing our weaknesses is as important as knowing
our strengths. Sometimes a weakness turns out to be
a strength, or at least to have a positive or "shadow"
side to it, and vice versa.

A very useful exercise is to identify strengths in
our weaknesses and weaknesses in our strengths.
For example, a person may see shyness as a weakness, but this can often be a quality to which others

are attracted. On the other hand, having an optimistic outlook on life is regarded as a strength, but sometimes this can lead to over-confidence or an inability to assess the true issues. A more pessimistic person can bring a realism to bear on circumstances. Like many other couples, we know this is true in our own relationship, because we are opposites in this respect! The more fully you understand yourself, the more fully you will be able to accept yourself and others.

## DEALING WITH WHAT WE DON'T LIKE ABOUT OURSELVES

All of us have things we don't like about ourselves, things we wish were different. Some of them relate to our *past* and our background. For example: You may have been an only child and wished you had been in a large family; you may have been brought up in a solo-parent family and realise how much you missed out on the love and companionship of the other parent; you may regret other difficult circumstances of childhood. There are always things we can look back on that we wish had been different, and sometimes people carry these as a grudge through life. Perhaps you feel resentful about things that have happened to you: hurtful experiences, broken relationships or missed opportunities.

Some of them relate to the *present*, such as: something about your body, your work, your living conditions, your personality, or your behaviour patterns. There may well be things about people you are related to, live with or work with that you don't like. Life may be a struggle for you at present. Some of them may relate to the *future*. For instance, you may have fears or the future may seem uninteresting, or even hopeless. You may have no clear direction for your life.

What can we do about these things? One very simple and effective way to start is by making a list of all the things you don't like about yourself and your circumstances, and to classify them under two headings:

| THINGS I CAN CHANGE. | THINGS I CAN'T CHANGE. |
|---|---|

*The things I can change* include my attitudes, beliefs, goals, behaviour patterns and even character traits. I may need some help from others and certainly from God. The limiting factor is often my lack of determination. Sometimes I can alter things that I don't like in my environment such as my work or living conditions. But these are more often outside my control. However, an inward change is always possible and is more lasting.

*The things I can't change* mainly relate to the past though some of them belong to the present. I certainly can't change somebody else, even someone I'm married to! It is wasted effort to try and it just makes things worse. *The only person I can change is myself*. The process can be seen more clearly in Figure 9.

*Handing them over*

Handing things over in our lives is not a passive process. It is sometimes difficult but always liberating. There are a number of ways we can do this:

1) **Acceptance**. Learning to accept things that we cannot change frees us from much stress and worry.

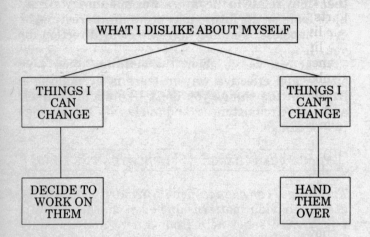

**Figure 9.** Dealing with what I don't like about myself

To accept things that have happened to us in the past rather than fight them or grow bitter about them is a sign of maturity. The famous prayer used by the Alcoholics Anonymous organisation puts this so well:

> "God grant me
> the serenity to accept the things I cannot change,
> the courage to change the things I can,
> and the wisdom to know the difference."[17]

2) **Changing attitudes**. In Chapter 6 we looked at distorted messages that have become fixed attitudes or "tapes" in our brain. Editing and changing destructive attitudes and beliefs is liberating. We can "erase" the old tape and "take on" the new.

3) **Prayer**. In a powerful way, we can "hand over" hurts and things we don't like about ourselves and our lives to God in prayer. It is helpful to write out the list of things we don't like about ourselves and cannot change, then burn the piece of paper. This symbolic act of burning the list says: "I refuse to be bound by them any more and I'm handing them over. I ask God to deal with them and set me free from their burden."

4) **Learning contentment**. Contentment is a quality we can develop. It is not a gift that some people are born with and others do not have, but it is a learned characteristic. St Paul said: "*I have learned* to be content whatever the circumstances. I know what it is to be in need, and I know what it is to have plenty. I have *learned the secret* of being content in any and every situation" (italics ours).[18]

Someone who has learned contentment is Helen. She is the eldest of five children and her mother died when she was young. As a teenager, just as life was opening up for her, Helen developed an illness which left her crippled with arthritis. This restricted her lifestyle and deprived her of the opportunity to fulfil her ambitions. But her indomitable spirit has enabled her to do many interesting and worthwhile things.

We have come to know and admire her in later life. She lives alone, but manages her little unit with minimal help from others. She is cut off from the outside world, only able to go out if taken by car or in a wheelchair. She says; "I never feel lonely. I have my books, radio, tapes, telephone, and my best Friend is always with me. What more do I need?" She expresses a positiveness and zest for life which reflects a deep contentment within.

5) **Forgiveness**. Forgiveness is the most powerful way to let go of hurts in the past. Our forgiveness not only frees others who may have hurt us, but more significantly, it releases us to wholeness and growth. The one who forgives receives more healing than the one who is forgiven. Forgiveness is an essential part of any inner healing process. It opens the door not only to personal health but to good relationships.

On the other hand, lack of forgiveness produces *resentment* and *bitterness* and leads to sickness of the body as well as the soul.[19] Studies have shown that unforgiveness actually inhibits our immune system and interferes with the defence mechanisms of the body. Thus the bitter, unforgiving person is more prone to illness.

Forgiveness is something Jesus talked about frequently. In fact, he taught that forgiveness by God is dependent on our forgiveness of others.[20] Forgiveness needs to become an attitude and a way of life, not just an isolated event. When Jesus told Peter he needed to forgive 490 times,[21] he did not say that it was necessarily for 490 different offences. Sometimes we may have to forgive the one offence repeatedly or affirm that we still forgive that person when the memory of the event comes back to our minds. It is not possible for us to "forgive and forget". Only God can do that.[22] We have to forgive and then choose not to recycle the hurtful memory. We can also choose to remember in order to rejoice in the healing that has taken place, because the hurt has been healed.

*What does forgiveness really mean?* The Oxford Dictionary defines it: "to pardon, remit, let off, cease to blame." The most commonly used Greek word translated in the New Testament as forgiveness is *"aphiemi"*, which means "to let the sin go, to send away". Jesus used this word on the cross as he forgave his murderers: "Father, forgive them, for they do not know what they are doing."[23] Jesus also taught us: "Forgive, and you will be forgiven."[24] Here the word is "*apoluo*" which means "to release, to loose away". In a real sense, *as we release others so we will be released.*

This is how one person dealt with his unforgiveness. Peter was the eldest in a family of four. As a little boy he idolised his father, but his dad never seemed to have any time for him. Dad was a real estate agent and trying to make a sale on a Saturday afternoon was higher up on his list of priorities than going fishing with his son. Peter sensed he was not very important to his father.

Peter's father also put him down a lot and kept telling him that he would not amount to much. Actually, Peter was talented musically and played the violin very well. His father never acknowledged his musical skills and frequently told him that he was a wimp because he showed no interest in football. When Peter was fourteen, his father walked out of their lives and went off to Australia with another woman.

Despite his academic and musical abilities, Peter saw himself as a failure. He felt rejected by his father and became very bitter about "the father that I never had". Later he married Julie, who came from a similar broken background. Three years later she had an affair with one of his best friends. This reinforced his sense of rejection, and his bitterness deepened. Peter and Julie really wanted to rebuild their marriage, but his anger and bitterness was like a brick wall in the way. Physically, Peter was unwell and very tense. He had lost over a stone in weight and was unable to sleep a full night without pills.

Peter admitted that he had never been able to forgive his father and realised that hatred and bitterness were destroying his life. He wanted to be free of this burden but did not know how. So we asked Peter to write a letter to his father, even though he had no idea where he was living. He was to include all the things that he had come to resent about him: the personal rejections, the put-downs he had received, and the shabby ways his mother was treated.

Peter read this letter aloud to his father, picturing him seated in a chair opposite. He offered his father forgiveness and also confessed his own negative attitude and bitterness and asked God's forgiveness for this. He then put a match to the letter, symbolising his letting go of it all. It may not have helped his father, but it certainly set Peter free from years of bitterness and resentment that had blocked his growth. Within a month he had regained his normal weight and started sleeping well without medication. He was now able to deal with the closer issue of forgiving his wife and asking her forgiveness for his part in what had happened. Peter also had to challenge and change his old rejection messages and negative "tapes" about himself that had built up over the years.

Forgiveness relieves emotional and spiritual blocks and frees us to change and grow. Growth may take time, but it cannot begin while we hold on to unforgiveness and blame others for what we are like.

## LOVE YOURSELF

Jesus said: "Love your neighbour as you love yourself." In chapter 5 we defined loving yourself as meaning: "to respect, honour, value, cherish, esteem and care for yourself". If we treat ourselves this way, we will be able to offer this kind of love to others. But you cannot give away what you do not have. Once I love myself, I can forget about myself and move on to fulfil the "new commandment" that Jesus gave us: "Love one another. As I have loved you, so you must love one another."[25]

The bottom rung in the ladder of learning to love yourself is to accept yourself, just as you are, the way God made you. To know that God accepts me totally gives me the right to accept myself. To receive his unconditional love for me gives me the courage to love what God loves so much.

However, the emphasis of Jesus' command to "Love your neighbour as you love yourself" is *to love your neighbour*. As we grow in our ability to love ourselves in a healthy way, so we are better able to love others. A beautiful example of this is recorded for us in the relationship between Jonathan and David. Jonathan was willing to set aside even his own rights as heir to the throne because of his love for David. And we are told that it was "because he loved him as he loved himself".[26]

Paul takes up this theme in his teaching on marriage in Ephesians chapter 5. If a man is married, his nearest neighbour is his wife. So Paul says: "Husbands ought to love their wives as their own bodies. He who loves his wife loves himself . . . each one of you also must love his wife as he loves himself" (vv 28,33). If I attempt to love my wife more than I love myself, I am really loving her less. If I love myself less than I love her, I make it so much harder for her to love me. The best gift anyone can bring to their marriage is healthy self-esteem.

# SUMMARY

Experiencing acceptance and learning to accept ourselves is the foundation on which we build a good self-esteem. This leads to a sense of belongingness in our world. Acceptance includes accepting and befriending our bodies as well as all our strengths and weaknesses. We can deal with the things we dislike about ourselves and hand over those that we cannot change. As we accept ourselves and rejoice in the way God loves and accepts us, so we can learn to love and forgive ourselves. Then we are free to love others as we love ourselves.

# A CREED OF SELF-AFFIRMATION

I believe that when God created me he did a
  good job.
    He looked at me and was very pleased.
I believe that I am made in the image of God.
    That image has been marred by sin,
    but there is a core of me which reflects
      God.
I believe that Christ died to release me
    to become the person he created me to be,
    and that he is at work in my life making
      this happen.
I believe that the things I see as blemishes,
    the things others may snigger at,
    God regards as part of my uniqueness.
I believe God loves me and that his love is
  unconditional,
    not depending on any virtue I may or may
      not possess,
    nor upon anything I have done or achieved.
    The Bible calls this grace; I call it amazing!
Though I cannot grasp the full extent of God's
  love for me,
    I accept it as so, and I rejoice in it.
      I thank God for myself,
    for what I am and for what I am becoming.

  Through Jesus Christ, the Lord,

                                    AMEN[27]

# REFLECTIONS AND EXERCISES

1 In your journal, head up three pages with the
  words:

QUALITIES
GIFTS
ACHIEVEMENTS

Under each heading list those things that apply to
you. For example:

QUALITIES:   You may be a loving, caring,
tolerant, honest, hard-work-
ing, patient, logical, generous . . . person.

GIFTS:     You may have practical, academic, musical, artistic,
mechanical . . . gifts.

ACHIEVEMENTS: You have made a good home,
built a good business, completed a course of training,
can cook . . . etc. Include *skills*
you have developed.

This exercise will help you to think of yourself with
"sober judgement".[28] Be as honest as possible and
include everything you can think of. If you run out
of ideas, get a friend to help you, who will no doubt
think of things you have omitted. Keep adding to
the list, at least one item each day to each page
for the next month.

*To acknowledge your gifts is to acknowledge the
Giver*, and not to acknowledge them is to ignore
the Giver. So this is not a brag list and can in fact
become a "Thankyou" list. Your qualities are who
you have become, by God's grace and your work.
Your achievements are what you have done with

the gifts you have been given, again with God's help. Acknowledging who you are in this way is not an artificial means of boosting a sagging ego, but a realistic affirmation of what you have been given and who you have become. To keep working on this exercise is a very practical way to strengthen your self-esteem. Share it with your partner, or a good friend. Don't stop adding to the list at the end of the month. If you are in a supportive group, share your lists with each other, not for discussion or analysis, but to affirm one another or to add items that have been overlooked.

2 Head up another page in your journal:

## I BELONG

Write down all the places you really feel you belong. For example:
I belong in my family ... I belong with my wife/husband ...
I belong to a church fellowship ... I belong to a sports club ...
I belong in a certain city/country ... I belong in the world ...
I belong to God ...

- Keep adding to this list as you think of groups or situations where you really feel comfortable. Share these together in your group.

3 Write down all the features you really appreciate about your body. Take the risk of asking a close friend to share with you what he or she appreciates about your body. You may be very pleasantly surprised! After all, others can see you better than you can see yourself.

4 Identify any regular symptoms you may be having. For example: Frequent headaches, migraines, pain in the neck or shoulders, abdominal colic or wind, sleep disturbance, mouth ulcers, skin rashes, allergies.

- Ask yourself these questions:

  "What is my body saying to me through this symptom?"
  "What might God be saying to me through my body?"
  "What can I do in response to this message?"

5 Head up two pages in your journal:

  STRENGTHS          GROWING AREAS

- Acknowledge your strengths. Thank God for them. Think about how you may be able to develop them further or use them more effectively for the benefit of others.
- Acknowledge your weaknesses. See them as *growing areas* in your life. God hasn't finished with you yet!

6 Spend some time thinking about strengths that are inherent in your weaknesses and weaknesses that lie behind your strengths, as described earlier in this chapter. For example:

- A stubborn person is also someone who does not give up easily.
- A strong-minded person is in danger of intolerance.

Doing this exercise in your group will produce some creative thinking.

7 Head up two pages in your journal:

## THINGS I DON'T LIKE ABOUT MYSELF THAT I CAN'T CHANGE

## THINGS I DON'T LIKE ABOUT MYSELF THAT I CAN CHANGE

*Things you can't change.* Work through the five ways of *handing over* what you don't like about yourself, which are described in this chapter. Maybe you need to:

- Learn to accept them.
- Change your attitude about them.
- Hand them over to God in prayer.
- Work on developing the quality of contentment.
- Practise forgiving.

*Things you can change.* Decide which of the ones on your list you need to work on first. Start with the easiest, because success there will encourage you with the others. Share the issue with someone who might be able to help you: perhaps your group, a close friend, a counsellor, a pastor. Team up with a person with whom you can pray about these things; who can encourage you as you make progress and to whom you can be accountable.

# NINE

# BE YOURSELF

*This above all – to thine own self be true,*
*and it must follow, as the night the day,*
*thou canst not then be false to any man.*[1]

William Shakespeare

As we grow in self-acceptance and learn to love ourselves it is possible to be ourselves in a natural way. We can now *forget* ourselves and relate to others authentically, without pretence or false modesty. Our relationships can be open without playing any psychological "games". People know when relating to you that what they see is what they get. The freedom to be yourself follows understanding, accepting and loving yourself. There is a beautiful little story of the Hassidic sage, Rav Zusia, who said: "In the world to come, I will not be asked, 'Why were you not Moses?', but, 'Why were you not Zusia?'"

Little children learn by copying others. Unfortunately, many people continue to imitate others all their lives instead of being themselves and becoming the persons God created them to be. This does not mean that we should not seek to develop characteristics that we admire in others, but these qualities must be real in us and not just a copy of someone else. In fact, St Paul defines the goal of the Christian life as becoming like Christ: "Become mature, attaining to the whole measure of the fulness of Christ . . ." ". . . so that we may present everyone perfect in Christ."[2] Becoming like Christ, can only happen as his qualities are formed in us through the work of the Holy Spirit. Then we can become models for others, as Paul was.[3]

"If you can think of anyone you would rather be than yourself you probably have a self-image problem."[4] It is a great relief to know that you do not have to be anyone but yourself! This brings a sense of freedom. You do not have to copy anyone but can focus your energies on truly becoming the person God created you to be. "Becoming like Christ" does not mean being a small imitation of the real thing but developing the "family likeness". We have five children, who are all very different from one another. But they also all have characteristics, often more noticeable to others, which clearly show that they are part of the same family.

Learning to be yourself is expressed in this little poem:

*The Plum*

> You should learn that you cannot be loved
>     by everyone.
>     You may be the finest plum in the world –
>     Ripe, juicy and succulent – and offer
>         yourself to all.
>     But there will be some people who do not
>         like plums.
> You must understand that if you are the
>         world's finest plum,
>     And someone you like doesn't happen to
>         like plums,

You have the choice of becoming a banana.
But you must be warned that if you choose
    to become a banana,
    You will be a second-rate banana.
    But you can always be the best plum.
You must also realise, if you choose to be a
    banana,
    There will be some people who do not like
    bananas.
Furthermore, you could spend your life
    Trying to become the best banana,
    Which is impossible, if you are a plum,

OR

You can seek again to be the best plum!

(Author unknown)

# ESTABLISH YOUR IDENTITY

Learning to be yourself begins with establishing your identity. This process starts at birth. Before birth, the developing child is an integral part of his/her mother. After birth, the child only gradually develops an awareness of being "apart" from mother and a separate individual. As the child discovers her own skin and body she begins to realise that mother is not part of that. At about six months, babies touch and explore their mother's face and often pull back to look intently at her in a growing awareness that they are different from her.[5] Another significant factor in the dawning of separateness is the feeling of hunger. The child associates discomfort and hunger with being alone and relying on another to meet these needs.[6]

Over the next few months, the child develops a sense of "otherness" and a self-identity which is separate from mother. Parents, especially mothers, can encourage this to develop in a healthy way or can slow it down. Some parents make this process of becoming independent very hard for their children. They *speak for* their children and make decisions *for* them instead of allowing them to do these things for themselves.

Sometimes a mother is afraid to encourage her children's independence because they are meeting her emotional needs. This is likely to happen if she is unfulfilled in her relationship with her husband, who should be the one to meet her emotional needs. Thus she may be very reluctant to cut the "umbilical cord", or "untie the apron strings", which join her to her children because she will feel abandoned.

In turn, this will make it harder for the children to develop good relationships with others, especially their future partners. They may leave home physically but not emotionally. This leaving process is essential before new relationships, especially marriage, can properly develop. God defined this process at the dawn of time: "For this reason a man will leave his father and mother and be united to his wife, and they will become one flesh."[7] So many couples have great difficulty in being "united" because one or other of them has not broken the emotional ties with one or both parents.

This "leaving" process not only means physically leaving the home of origin and parental authority, it goes much deeper. It involves leaving or re-thinking parental values, attitudes and behaviours. We may retain wish to many of these, but it is far better when this is through *choice* rather than from habit. In marriage, a husband and wife both need to evaluate their "parent messages" so that they can determine together whether these are right for them as a couple. Until we have "left" our family modelling in this way, we are not fully independent.

Single people, who never marry, can also struggle with this problem of not leaving their parent's authority. Dorothy was fifty-six and the very efficient secretary of a large institution. Although she liked her job, she had a constant sense of unfulfilment in her life, and lacked a feeling of self-worth. Dorothy and her younger sister were born when their parents were in their early forties. Both her parents were very controlling and she was seldom allowed to make her own decisions. Her friends were all carefully screened, and even into her late teens Mother decided for her what dress she should wear when she went out. Dad found her first job for her in a bank. When she was eighteen Dorothy fell madly in love with an older married man and became pregnant by him. She wanted to keep the child but her mother would not hear of it because this would bring shame on the family. So to please her mother she had him adopted.

Her younger sister rebelled against the parental domination, left home as soon as she had a job, and eventually married and moved to another town. But Dorothy continued to live at home. After her father died she cared for her mother until she died. Dorothy had some relationships with men over the years which could have led to marriage, but her mother succeeded in sabotaging these. Even after her parents passed on, she felt as if their ideas were still influencing her and found it hard to make decisions. Beneath a submissive mask Dorothy was seething with anger. Eventually, she was able to express this and then "talk" to her mother. In a counselling session she was asked to imagine her mother seated in another chair opposite[8] and to tell her the things she had never been able to express to her when she was alive, both positive and negative. Only then was Dorothy able to forgive her parents and to ask for God's forgiveness for the wrong choices she had made. She worked through the grief of losing her son and of never being able to marry.

Over the next few months, Dorothy grew as a person. She learned to accept herself and even to like herself. For the first time she felt *free to be herself* and to express her opinions at work and in her relationships. She still had to deal with some of her "parent messages". But as these surfaced, she had the confidence to challenge, evaluate and change them where necessary. Dorothy developed a real desire to grow and become the person God had created her to be.

## CELEBRATE YOUR UNIQUENESS

In Chapter 5 we tried to express something of the "wonder of being me". Each one of us is an incredibly complex and wonderful creation. But there is more. Even though there are about 5 billion people in the world in which we live, and billions more who have lived and died, not one of them is exactly like you or me. *You are special*, right down to your fingerprints. You have your own genetic make-up and DNA pattern. Your voice and your handwriting can be identified as different from that of anyone else. You have a unique personality, your own mix of emotions and talents and your own way of seeing life. It can be truly said: "When God made you, he broke the mould!"

Some years ago, on one of the Queen's visits to New Zealand, a ceramic artist was asked to create a native bird in fine pottery to be presented as a gift to the Queen. Actually, he made two of them, exquisitely designed and identical. Then he smashed one in order to enhance the value of the other. This symbolic act meant that the gift to the Queen would be unique, the only one of its kind in the world.

This is how God regards you. You are the only one in the world exactly like you. This enhances your value and worth to him. It also means that there is no one else in the world who can glorify God in precisely the same way as you can. He has a specific design for your life and a distinctive task for you to do. You may not feel that you have "arrived", and hopefully you never will. God has not finished with any of us yet. The beautiful sculptures of Michelangelo were once shapeless blocks of marble, each one different but unfinished. Each of us is one of God's unfinished masterpieces. As we discover our uniqueness, then we can have confidence to be who we are. We no longer need to rely on others for our identity and worth, as expressed in a little poem:

> If I am I because I am I,
> And You are You because You are You,
>   Then I am and You are.
> But if I am I because You are You,
> And You are You because I am I,
>   Then I am not and You are not.

> Rabbi Mendel of Kotsk (1787–1859)

*Sincerity* is the mark of real people who know who they are, value themselves and endeavour to be who they are. The origin of the word sincere is interesting. It comes from the Latin "sine cere", meaning "without wax". In those days it was common to have statuettes or idols in the homes. Sometimes shopkeepers would repair small chips in the marble icon with wax, which may not have been apparent until after the purchase had been made. Hence, the importance of ensuring the article was "without wax", i.e. intact and with nothing to hide. Paul uses this metaphor when he prays for the Christians at Philippi, that they will be "sincere and without offence".[9]

*Uniqueness* has very significant implications for Christians. If God has created each of us different from everyone else in gifting and personality, it follows that he has a special job for each to do.[10] John Powell expresses this idea in his own inimitable style:

> A special piece of God's truth has been placed in your hands, and God has asked you to share it with the rest of us. The same is true of me. And just as you are the one and only you, your truth is given to you alone. No one else can tell the world your truth or bestow on others your act of love. Only you have all the requirements to be and do what you are to be and do.[11]

# WHO YOU ARE, NOT WHAT YOU DO

If you ask a young child, "What are you going to be when you grow up?", typical replies would be: A fireman, an engine driver, a nurse, or a policeman. At a very early age we learn to equate what we are with what we do. Then at the other end of life, some people almost stop living when they retire or are unable to achieve any more: "Last year I was a bank manager ... now I am nothing." What we are may determine what we do, but what *we are is far more than what we do*. What we do *affects* who we are, but that is not who we are. Someone has said, most of us are human DOings, not human BEings! A healthy self-esteem enables us to sort out the difference between these two aspects of our lives.

In God's kingdom, the rewards are not for achievement but for character. The truly spiritual person is not the one who manifests the "gifts of the Spirit",[12] but the *"fruit* of the Spirit": "Love, joy, peace, patience, kindness, goodness, faithfulness, gentleness and self-control."[13] St Paul said that even if he had the gifts of tongues, prophecy and knowledge, or died the death of a martyr, it would all amount to nothing if he were not a loving person.[14] Nothing can give a greater sense of self-worth than to allow one's roots to "go down deep into the soil of God's marvellous love"[15] and to "grow up in every way into [Christ]."[16]

At the end of thirty years of *being* and not doing, God said about Jesus: "This is my Son, whom I love; with him I am well pleased."[17] This is what God thought of him for who he was, *before* he had achieved anything significant in human terms. He had not been to university, preached a sermon, performed a miracle, written a book or done anything outstanding. Certainly he had cared for his widowed mother and family until he was thirty, and was a skilled carpenter. But he was a "nobody" from a remote village in the outer reaches of the Roman Empire. If we had been writing his biography, we would probably have kept this statement for the final accolade after an outstanding life of achievement – after Jesus had accomplished the great work of salvation.

God's commendation of his Son shows that who we *are* matters more to him than what we do. So our task is to truly *be* who we are and to *become* the people he created us to be. "Become what thou art."[18] To rely on what we own or what we do for our sense of self-worth is the attitude of the world, which is completely opposite to God's way. The Apostle John makes this abundantly clear: "For everything in the world – the cravings of sinful man, the lust of his eyes and the boasting of what he has and does – comes not from the Father but from the world."[19]

Perhaps the most obvious way in which we express who we are is in our speech, so it is important to be able to do this effectively.

# SPEAK FOR YOURSELF

Attitudes to ourselves can be revealed by the language we use. Many people think and speak in the third person and thus depersonalise themselves. They frequently use the words "you", "we", "they" or "it" when they really mean "I". When we were young, we were taught to use the word "one" rather than "I", because to say "I" was regarded as being egotistical! This is not necessarily true. In rather subtle ways listed below we can make ourselves into objects rather than subjects.

But when we speak for ourselves we feel much better about ourselves, and other people will pay more attention to what we say. This is part of "being yourself". Of course, it is also risky to express the truth about ourselves and safer to speak objectively. But to own our statements is being authentic and lets people know what we are feeling. This will improve both our communication and our relationships. Here are some typical examples of speaking as an object or a subject:

| *Being an object* | *Being a subject* |
| --- | --- |
| "You don't understand me." | "I don't feel understood." |
| "One doesn't like to take risks." | "I'm cautious." |
| "It's too difficult." | "I can't do it." |
| "You don't know which way to turn." | "I'm confused." |
| "We like it when we're together." | "I like being with you." |

(For further examples see exercise 5 at the end of the chapter.)

People who wish to be themselves must clarify their language and speak for themselves. Speaking for yourself is a great help in learning to be yourself. But so often our language is either defensive or aggressive in response to what someone else says or does. In other words, we *react* to other people, without making a clear decision first as to what our response to them will be.

## ACT, DON'T REACT

Part of being yourself is determining to live as an *actor* rather than a *reactor*. An actor in this sense means someone who takes the initiative, not someone who acts a part. While it is acknowledged that some personality types, particularly introverts, might find this harder than others, this is a life skill we can all develop.

**Actors** accept responsibility for their lives and take the initiative. They have clear values they wish to live by. They make decisions based on thought-out priorities rather than merely responding to what is urgent or expedient. They reach out to form relationships and will try to mend those that have been broken.

**Reactors** wait for things to happen before making decisions and usually watch things happen rather than make them happen. They tend to react to circumstances and situations negatively or defensively. Their lives are often filled with activity and routine to which they respond automatically. Reactors often feel caught up in the "rat race"; being driven rather than in the driver's seat. They often regard themselves as "victims" in their relationships and powerless to make changes.

Actors do not react to circumstances and situations, they respond to them *pro-actively*. Their responses come from choices they are making, rather than being reflex actions over which they have no control. For example, if actors are being abused, instead of reacting in kind and hurling abuse back, they can say to themselves: "I'm bigger than this", or "Nobody is going to determine my behaviour for me". They may not be in charge of the situation but they are in charge of themselves. Jesus behaved like this.[20] So did Paul.[21] Being an actor rather than a reactor does not come naturally to us but the Holy Spirit can develop this response in us.

Probably all of us can identify with being a reactor at times. In our own experience, we can certainly relate to this and we find that often we have to monitor what is happening in our lives: "Are we acting or reacting in this situation or in this relationship?" The most effective way to become an actor is to *build space into our lives*, preferably each day, when we take time out to evaluate what is going on. Time to be quiet. Time to pray. Time to meditate. Time to listen to what God is saying to us. Henri Nouwen puts it: "When we believe that we are created in the image of God and come to realise that Christ came to reimage this, then meditation and prayer lead us to our true identity."[22]

Involving God in the details of my life and seeking his will does not make me a reactor or a robot. The very decision to hand over my life to him is a positive action. God does not want to stop us from acting. On the contrary, he provides the strength and wisdom that we need to become effective actors. When I handed over my life to Christ, he did not take over the "driver's seat". He graciously responded to my invitation to become the "Navigator". I still have to do the driving and make decisions, but can now draw on his wisdom, guidance and power St Paul said: "I can do everything through him who gives me strength."[23] Notice that Paul is still the "actor" here, but with new energy. Christ does not take away our initiative, but comes alongside as our companion and guide. We still have to make the choices and do the work but we are no longer alone. This balance is hard to find and comes with maturity and growth in the Christian life.

Being an "actor" in life requires maturity. It means avoiding aggressiveness or arrogance on the one hand and passivity or timidity on the other. The proper balance between these two is called assertiveness.

# ASSERTIVENESS

All of us behave in one of three ways. Throughout the day we act passively, assertively or aggressively. It is perhaps best to think of it as a continuum of behaviour:

PASSIVE............ASSERTIVE............AGGRESSIVE

## Passive

Passive behaviour includes not accepting responsibility for your life, ignoring your feelings and not speaking for yourself. Living behind a mask, hiding behind a role and not being real is to live passively. Passive people find it hard to accept themselves or to acknowledge their strengths and weaknesses. They will frequently put themselves down or withdraw into shyness. They are likely to become closed off or people who find it hard to make relationships. Passive people tend to find their satisfaction in life as workaholics. They find it hard to say "No" and may become "martyrs". In other words, passive behaviour typifies low self-esteem.

## Aggressive

Aggressive behaviour is at the opposite end of the continuum. Aggressive people like to control others and frequently put others down. They are usually dogmatic, rigid thinkers and seldom trust others. Maintaining close relationships is very hard for them. They tend to dominate a group and be the centre of attention. Aggressive people are the "go-getters" of this world who will push others out of the way to achieve their goals. They are often very angry people. Aggressive people appear to have a lot of confidence, but as was pointed out in Chapter 4, these behaviours often hide a deep insecurity and cover up low self-esteem.

## Assertive

Assertive behaviour is the true alternative to both passive and aggressive behaviour. Some people who are aware of being passive attend assertiveness courses. While they may learn some useful skills, they can also move from being passive to aggressive! This happens if the basic issue of self-esteem is not addressed. Only when we have developed a healthy self-esteem can we be truly assertive without being aggressive or self-centred. Healthy verbal assertiveness is a skill that many adults have to learn because few of us have observed good models of assertive behaviour in our childhood. "True assertiveness is a way of being in the world which confirms one's individual worth and dignity while simultaneously confirming and maintaining the worth of others."[24]

Assertive people are aware of themselves. They are in touch with their needs and feelings and are able to express these appropriately, without being controlled by them. True assertion follows learning to accept yourself, and indeed to love yourself, so that you can forget about yourself and reach out to others in a positive and open way. Assertiveness means interacting with others with confidence and caring. Assertive people do not push others around, nor do they allow themselves to be pushed around or manipulated by others.

Jesus demonstrated assertiveness in his life on earth. He showed us how to be real as individuals and in our relationships. His gentleness has some-times been presented as passivity, but there was nothing passive or "meek and mild" about the way he confronted the religious leaders of the day.[25] The story of his trial before Annas models true assertiveness. After Jesus had replied to a question, one of the bystanders struck him on the face and demanded: "Is that any way to answer the high priest?" Jesus replied in a direct, assertive manner: "If I said something wrong, testify as to what is wrong. But if I spoke the truth, why did you strike me?"[26]

Assertiveness is being neither passive nor aggressive but fully authentic. It is not a lifestyle we decide to adopt, but it flows out of knowing ourselves and feeling good about who we are. It is evidence of good self-esteem.

# WINNERS AND LOSERS

In their book *Born To Win*, Muriel James and Dorothy Jongeward describe the concept of being a "winner" or a "loser". They define a winner as: "One who responds authentically by being credible, trustworthy, responsive and genuine, both as an individual and as a member of society. A loser is someone who fails to respond authentically."[27] This differs from the normal concept of winning and losing, in which a person who wins automatically turns the other competitors into losers. But in this sense, a winner is winning in life and, in fact, is more likely to help losers to win. In the terms of what we are saying, a "winner" corresponds to someone with a healthy self-esteem and a "loser" has poor self-esteem.

To help contrast "winners" and "losers", the common characteristics of each are contrasted below. Items marked (B) are concepts drawn from the book *Born to Win* and items marked (H) are ideas from the book *Winners and Losers*.[28] Reading through this list may help clarify some of the things we have said in earlier chapters.

| | WINNERS | LOSERS |
|---|---|---|
| (B) | Strive for authenticity. | Achievement is their main aim. |
| (B) | Able to reveal themselves. | Live mainly behind masks. |
| | Care about people. | Care mostly about themselves. |
| (H) | Listen to others. | Wait their turn to talk. |
| | Can accept others. | Need to control others. |
| | Assess people's actions. | Judge others' intentions. |
| | Can give and receive love. | Find both difficult. |
| (H) | Give more than they take. | Take more than they give. |
| (B) | In touch with their feelings. | Afraid to face their feelings. |
| | Able to express their feelings. | Smoulder; repress feelings. |
| (B) | Responsible for their lives. | Make excuses; blame others. |
| | Believe we make life. | Trust in luck. |
| | Face problems. | Try to avoid problems. |
| | Can accept criticism. | Must be right. |
| | Able to apologise | Try to find scapegoats. |
| (H) | Make commitments. | Make promises. |
| (H) | Admit their prejudices. | Deny any prejudices. |
| (H) | Learn from their mistakes. | Stop trying new ways. |
| | Make time to do things. | Never have enough time. |
| (B) | Kill time. | Live fully here and now. |
| | Acknowledge both their strengths and weaknesses. | Minimise or deny both. |
| | Sympathetic towards weakness. | Intolerant of others' weaknesses. |
| | Can laugh at themselves. | Find it easier to laugh at others. |
| | Act decisively. | React to situations. |
| (B) | Spontaneous and creative. | Rigid thinkers. |
| (H) | Turn deficits into assests. | Turn assets into deficits. |
| | Live out who they are. | Imitate others. |
| | Guided by the important. | Controlled by the urgent. |
| | Able to be assertive. | Usually passive or aggressive |
| | Concerned with BEING. | Preoccupied mostly in DOING. |

### Things they say:

| | | |
|---|---|---|
| | "Life's great!" | "Nothing goes my way." |
| (H) | "Let's find out." | "Nobody knows." |
| | "I could do better." | "I'm not so bad as others." |
| | "Why not?" | "Why should I?" |
| | "Good morning, God!" | "Good God, morning." |

# SELF-ESTEEM AND WHOLENESS

The journey to wholeness is God's purpose for all of us. A *whole person* is not perfect but someone who is growing in all areas of his or her life: physically, intellectually, emotionally, socially and spiritually. It is possible to be physically mature and intellectually capable but emotionally stunted and socially inept. Emotionally mature people may still be spiritually dead. On the other hand, a spiritually alive individual can be intellectually or emotionally immature. Jesus modelled for us a human being who grew to maturity in all these areas. "Jesus grew in wisdom and stature, and in favour with God and men."[29] Paul defined our goal as: ". . . [to] become *mature*, attaining to the whole measure of the fulness of Christ" (italics ours).

Healthy self-esteem significantly affects three main areas of life in particular: our self-awareness, our ability to make relationships and our spiritual growth. Figure 10 illustrates this.

## Self-Awareness

A healthy sense of self-worth gives me the desire to know myself better and the courage to deal with areas within myself that are not healthy. Clearly, the more I know who I am the more I will be free to work towards becoming the person God created me to be, i.e. fully alive and fully myself. The more self-aware I am the more I will be aware of others and open to God-awareness.

## Relationships

Without good self-esteem, meaningful relationships with others are difficult and I will find it hard to be

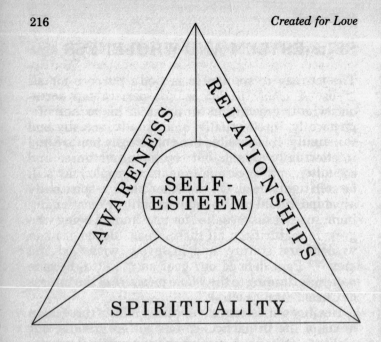

**Figure 10.** Self-esteem and wholeness.

open and intimate. But with a good sense of self-worth, I am no longer preoccupied with myself so can reach out with love to others. Two people with good self-esteem can nurture one another. Healthy relationships with others presuppose, and are dependent on, a healthy relationship with myself. A true relationship with God includes a good relationship with others also.[30]

## *Spirituality*

True spirituality is not based on a belief system but on a love relationship between the individual and God. For any real relationship to take place, both parties must know who they are and be able to share who they are with one another. Martin Buber calls this the "I–Thou encounter".[31] God has made encounter with himself possible through Jesus Christ, and in fact longs for it to take place far more than we do. Discovering how much God loves me and how significant I am to him encourages me to keep on growing in my relationship with him.

Healthy self-esteem is thus an important part of our self-awareness, our ability to make good relationships and to mature spiritually.

## SUMMARY

Becoming the person God created me to be is one way of describing the purpose for living. We have to learn how to express who we are authentically, both in our language and in our behaviour. This involves taking the initiative in life and being an actor rather than a reactor. Expressing who we are to the world takes courage. "The courage to be is rooted in the God who appears when God has disappeared in the anxiety of doubt."[32] Who we are is God's gift to us; who we become is our gift to God.

# REFLECTIONS AND EXERCISES

1 To what degree do you think you have become independent from your parents in your thinking, attitudes and reactions? Write down in your journal any "parent messages" that you still have not challenged or thought through as an adult. Spend some time reflecting on these.

2 Make a list in your journal of the special ways in which you differ from your family and friends. These may relate to your personal qualities, gifts and talents or physical characteristics. Together these make up your individuality.

   • Spend some time rejoicing in your uniqueness and thanking God for making you the way you are.
   • Share your new awarenesses in your small group.

3 Are there any areas of your life where you have applied some "wax" to conceal deficiencies? Reflect on the degree to which you are sincere and genuine? Start by praying these prayers: Psalm 26:2; Psalm 139:23–24.

4 Spend some time meditating on Galatians 5:22. To what extent do you see these fruits of the Spirit growing in your life? Which ones in particular need to be developed?

   • Share this with a close friend. You can provide a "mirror" for each other. This could also be done in your small group.

5 Practice being a "subject" not an "object" in your speech. This is a good exercise to do as a group,

where you can check on each other. For example, turn the following statements into "I" messages which clearly state the speaker's own feelings or need.

"You know how it feels when people don't understand you."
"You make me angry."
"It's time you started listening to me."
"One can't be sure if it is true."
"It's terrible to feel all alone."
"They don't let me be myself around here."
"It's hard trying to do all the work on your own."
"You make me happy."
"You are driving too fast."
"Lord, please will you help me to love you."

(For suggested changes see References and Notes, Chapter 9:note 33.)

- Continue to monitor your speech. Give permission to members of your group to point out to you whenever you speak objectively about yourself instead of subjectively. Take note of the times when speaking as a subject (using "I" statements) has helped your communication or interaction with others.

6 Are you an "Actor" or a "Reactor"?

- Identify some times in the past few days when you have reacted to people rather than acting out of reality and integrity. Why do you think you behaved that way? How could you have acted differently?
- Are you an *initiator* or *responder* in your relationships? Do you seek to mend broken

relationships or leave it to others to sort
it out?
- How defensive are you when someone criti-
  cises you or points out a deficiency? Do you
  react negatively or are you able to hear and
  evaluate what they have said and respond
  appropriately?
- Do you feel driven by your work? Do your commitments run you or do you control them?

7 Mark X on the line below to indicate where you
think you usually are on this continuum:

PASSIVE          ASSERTIVE          AGGRESSIVE

- Ask your friends, or the other members of your
  group, if they see you in the position where
  you have placed your mark.

8 To assess your assertiveness, how would you
respond in these situations? Discuss them in your
group and think of other scenarios that might be
more related to your life at present.

a) You are in a restaurant, in the "No Smok-
ing" section, and someone near you lights up a
cigarette.
b) You have a visitor who stays very late talking
about inconsequential things. You are tired and
have to get up early for a busy day ahead.
c) You are asked to give a talk at a group because
they can't find another speaker. It is at a busy
time for you and you have other important things
to do.
d) A friend of yours is about to make a decision
which appears to you to be very unwise.

e) You have been unjustly criticised for something you did not do, or the wrong inference taken from what you said.

f) Your friend/partner keeps doing something that annoys you.

g) You are interrupted by someone in a group while you are making a contribution that you consider important.

h) A Christian friend is doing something which is clearly wrong or sinful. What action would you take?

# TEN

# REVEAL YOURSELF

*I cannot know myself except through the intermediacy of another person.*

Jean-Paul Sartre, 1905–1980

In the last three chapters we have focused on understanding yourself, learning to fully accept and love yourself and on being yourself. Who you are and who you are becoming, are more important than what you do. True assertiveness is being able to express what you think or feel to others without apologising for it or being aggressive.

*We have been created for love.* This capacity to love is stimulated and brought to life when we *experience* love. The Apostle John, an expert on love, tells us: "We love because [God] first loved us."[1] It is only because of God's great love that we are capable of love. People who do not know God have not yet discovered how much God loves them. When we are overwhelmed by how much God loves us, our natural response is to love him. God communicated his love to us by *revealing* himself to us through his prophets and ultimately in his Son, Jesus.[2] In the same way, we truly love others as we reveal who we are to them. This encourages them to respond to us in love.

It is also true that *as we reveal ourselves* to others so we discover more about who we are and can learn to love ourselves. "We become fully conscious only of what we are able to express to someone else."[3] The best way to grow in self-esteem is to reveal yourself to at least one other person. Some personalities may find it harder than others to reveal themselves to another person. But it is still a principle of life.

Self-esteem is a *relational* function. If you lived by yourself on a desert island a low self-esteem would not be too much of a handicap. But because we live in relationships, low self-esteem is a great disadvantage. "We can never have a positive self-image apart from other people."[4] Not only do we need a good self-esteem to be able to relate well to others, it is in the revealing of ourselves to others, and to God, that we grow in self-esteem.

Many people have never revealed who they are to another person. They live as islands. This can happen even in a marriage. In fact, many couples could be described like this:

> I live on an island
> and he lives on an island,
> and neither of us can swim!

One of the ways in which people maintain their "island status" is by wearing masks.

## MASKS

All of us have learned to hide behind masks and some people even live behind them. Masks cover up the things that we do not like about ourselves or do not want other people to see in us. In Chapter 7 we described the difference between the "person" and the "personage". My personage is my self-picture, which is often a distortion of who I really am. If I constantly live in my personage rather than my person, I will be living a role rather than being real. We use masks to help us live in roles.

*Some common masks*

Masks are similar to the "labels", "T-shirt messages" and "compensating behaviours" that we talked about in Chapter 4. People wear different masks for different situations, but usually have a favourite one to wear at times when they are insecure or do not feel good about themselves. Here are some masks that you may recognise in yourself or others:

**Successful Steven** had it all together. He was a capable businessman and let people know it by the designer clothes he wore, the personalised number plate on his expensive car and his way of assuming that he should take control of every conversation. It was important to him not only to succeed but to be *seen* as a success. Steven worked long hours and had little time for people, even his family. He shared none of his feelings or anxieties with his wife. In fact, she even had to ring his secretary to know what his plans and movements were!

What people did not know about Steven was that he was *desperately lonely*. He had never had a close friend in his life nor had he ever experienced true intimacy with anybody, as a child or as an adult. He was scared to get close to people because they might discover that he did not "have it all together" after all. Inside a successful man of forty was a frightened boy of fourteen.

**Sally Super-mum** was the envy of many. Her magnificent home always looked so tidy when visitors came, with not even a cushion out of place. She had three well-scrubbed children who did what they were told. Sally even had time to go to work, so that they could afford to send their children to private schools. She always dressed as if she had just stepped out of a fashion magazine. As well as being a very active member of her church she was also involved in a variety of charities.

What people did not know about Sally was that she was *so tired of living like this*. She longed to step off the merry-go-round and enjoy life just a little. But if she was seen as not quite "perfect", this would be devastating to her sense of self-worth.

**Marion Martyr** had a hard life and she certainly gave that impression. Her husband was a busy minister, at the beck and call of everyone in the parish, except Marion. He was often away for special meetings around the country. But she had accepted her lot and shouldered her job of being virtually a "solo-parent" to their four children without complaining. She also spent a lot of time baking for others and visiting needy people. She had not had a proper holiday since they were married, because to save money they always rented a cottage, where Marion still had to do all the cooking and housework.

What people did not know about Marion was that she longed for others to *consider her needs*, or even to notice that she had some! But when anyone tried to do something for her, she would decline the offer and tell them she was coping. She "hated to be a burden to anybody" and did not believe that she deserved to be loved. If someone did her a favour, she had to return it. She did not think that she was worth very much and spent her life trying to earn respect and love, but seldom received it.

**Charlie Cool** was a popular person. He was always cheerful and nothing was too much trouble for Charlie. In fact, he could never say "No" to a request for help, even if he had more important things to do. He was a successful salesman, but never really exerted himself in his job or took anything very seriously. He had a lot of "mates" but no close friends. People liked having Charlie around and he was always good for a laugh at a party.

What people did not know about Charlie was that under his cheerful exterior was a very *sad person*. He had decided very early in life that he was not as capable as his two older brothers, so he set about getting his needs met by being liked. He was always the "clown" or focus of attention in a group. This made him feel good for a while, but he really wished people would take him seriously. However, his behaviour made quite sure that no one could get close enough to him to find out how he really felt.

**Ruth Rescuer** was a lovely person, kind and gentle. She was the eldest of a large family and her mother had relied on her to help bring up the younger children. Ruth was a natural peacemaker and even as a little girl would help settle other children's quarrels. She often collected "lame ducks" and looked after people who needed help. There was never a shortage of these! She seldom considered her own needs or took time out to care for herself. She married an inadequate man whom she helped recover from alcoholism, but he was incapable of holding down a job for very long. Ruth became a co-dependent. She went out to work as well as bringing up three young children, in order to survive. What people did not know about Ruth was that she was *tired* *of being strong for everyone else.* She longed for someone to meet a few of her needs. But no one knew what her needs were, as Ruth conveyed the impression that she did not have any. Because she was always the strong one, nobody saw the hurting little girl inside.

## The use and abuse of masks

Masks have their uses, especially out in the hard world. Without them we would be needlessly hurt. Masks and roles may be useful in a work situation, or when we are with strangers who do not need to know and probably would not care about what we are feeling. But masks are totally inappropriate in the intimacy of marriage and family life. Those who really know us well can see past our masks anyway! So why bother to wear them? They keep loved ones at a distance and interfere with honest communication and the development of intimacy. They prevent us from making healthy relationships.

The other place where masks are inappropriate is in the church family. Unfortunately, it is tempting to wear our brightest and best "Christian mask" at church. We may be hurting and discouraged inside but afraid of being a "bad witness". We like to be seen as a success by our Christian friends. It is possible to go to meetings without really "meeting" anyone! This is usually the result of relating "mask to mask" instead of person to person and is contrary to the essence of true body-life and fellowship.

The obvious answer is to drop my mask when it is inappropriate, such as in an intimate relationship. By taking off my mask I will show you what I am really like. But that is scary, especially if I do not like what I think is behind my mask. If I show you who

I am, what will you do with that information? Will you ridicule, disbelieve, dislike, blame or reject me? Perhaps you will tell others what I have shared with you. This is why so few people are able to remove their masks, even in marriage. To take such a risk, I need firstly to feel safe with you, but I also need to feel secure about myself.

# CASTLES

Another useful metaphor is to think in terms of each one of us living inside a castle. By the time we are adults our castle walls are thick and strong. We may have been hurt badly as children and needed these defences then to survive. The walls of some people's castles are about six feet thick, made of reinforced concrete and surrounded by a moat of water! They have become isolated castles and no one is allowed in, nor does the person ever come out.

But each castle has a drawbridge, which is under the control of the owner of the castle. This access can be lowered but the chains may be rusty, as they have seldom been used. However, it is less risky to lower my drawbridge than to remove a mask, because it can be done more slowly and is under my control. I can always raise it again if there are any signs of danger.

When two people lower their drawbridges to one another, they can walk across and meet. They can even invite each other into their castles; discover each other and, in fact, discover themselves at the same time. It is in this real encounter with at least one other person that we can grow best in our self-esteem. But how is this emotional dialogue achieved?

# REVEALING YOURSELF

*The Johari window* is a well known model for understanding ourselves and showing how we can reveal ourselves. (It was first described by *Joe* Luft and *Harry* Ingram,[5] hence the name "Johari".) The whole window represents ourselves. The four panes that we are looking through, as it were, are four aspects of our personality. These four panes are not the same size in reality. The fourth one is much larger than the others.

I) The first pane refers to my OPEN or public self. It is the part of me that I am very much aware of and is also obvious to others, i.e. known to self and known to others (see Figure 11). It includes for example, my gender, size and other visible physical features; what I do in life; how I present myself to the world.

II) The second pane represents my HIDDEN self, hidden that is *to me*. It refers to my "blind spots",

|  | Known to Self | Not Known to Self |
|---|---|---|
| Known to Others | I.<br>**OPEN**<br>(Public self) | II.<br>**HIDDEN**<br>(Blind self) |
| Not Known to Others | III.<br>**SECRET**<br>(Private self) | IV.<br>**UNKNOWN**<br>(Buried self) |

**Figure 11.** The Johari Window

sometimes known as "bad-breath areas"! These are
aspects of myself which I am not aware of but are
things that others recognise, especially people who
know me well. For example, I may have mannerisms
or speak in ways of which I am unaware. A person
may come across as insensitive or a snob to others
and be oblivious to the impression his mannerisms
are creating.

**III)** The third pane is my SECRET or "private"
self. This refers to parts of me that I deliberately
*hide*. They are things that are known to me but not to
others. These include my fears, failures, weaknesses,
hurts, dreams, ambitions and especially my feelings.
They are things that I am sensitive about, ashamed
of or possibly things that give me secret delight. They
include positive things about myself, perhaps parts
of my vision for the future that I have never revealed
to anyone and never had the courage to explore.

Many people hide their feelings. In Caucasian,
Northern European cultures and also in Asia it is
not considered appropriate to express feelings. It
is particularly common for men to cover up their
feelings in Western society, where an expression of
feelings is regarded as evidence of weakness. After
a few years of repressing feelings, a man may find
it difficult even to be aware of his feelings, let alone
share them. In New Zealand, for example, the only
feeling that is regarded as an appropriate "male"
one is anger. Other feelings, such as fear, confusion,
sadness and depression are repressed or covered up
by most men. Boys are taught, often by their mothers
as well as their fathers, that "big boys don't cry".
They learn to "keep a stiff upper lip". Even joy and
expressions of happiness are "not cool", except when
watching sport!

This makes emotional dialogue very difficult for men. They have been conditioned out of it. It doesn't matter in the world of business, where giving away one's feelings could be a disadvantage. The problem comes when males try to make close relationships with women, who are usually good at sharing feelings, or even with other males. Feelings are the raw materials with which close relationships are built. This is especially important in marriage. If a man is unable to share at a feeling level this will lead to frustration in their relationship because of their different desired levels of intimacy. Because the wife is usually so much better at sharing feelings, this may cause her husband to "pull up his draw-bridge" even higher. The more she clamours to get inside "his castle", the more he closes up.

We cover up with masks things we find hard to own or to express. We often do not want others to see us as we really are. For example, a man who is by nature gentle and tender may present a tough macho image. A woman who is very bright and intelligent may have learned to wear a mask of not showing too much initiative because others, especially the men in her life, find this threatening. A person who is insecure often wears a mask of confidence and bravado. Someone who is lonely and afraid of taking the risks involved in close relationships, may present as being self-sufficient and independent. Those who have been badly hurt in the past may hide completely inside their castle.

**IV** The fourth pane is my UNKNOWN self. This is sometimes called the buried self or the *subconscious*. It represents the deeper parts of my personality that are unknown to me, and certainly unknown to others. It includes things that I have buried and "forgotten", such as childhood hurts, traumas and rejections from the past. It could be such things as emotional, physical or sexual abuse, which a young child was unable to cope with at the time that it happened, so it became buried in the subconscious.

Included in this area are what the Bible calls the "heart" and my "old self".[6] These parts of my life will not be apparent until the Holy Spirit opens my mind. It is hard to become aware of some aspects of the "unknown" self on our own. At times, deep personal sharing with a friend may give insight into some of them. Other processes such as psychotherapy, psychodrama, dream analysis and the use of drawing may be very helpful in providing access to the "unknown self".

## Emotional dialogue

How can we become more open people, understand ourselves better and grow in self-esteem? The process of emotional dialogue provides the key (see Figure 12). This takes place when two people who

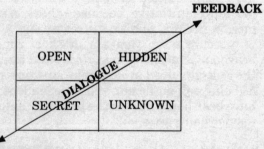

**Figure 12.** The Dialogue Process

trust each other are prepared to be open with one another and share at an emotional level. They are not talking superficially now but saying something about their inner selves. They drop their masks, come out of their castles and truly meet each other.

When this happens, I will disclose some of my "secret" self to this person and she or he will do the same to me. As trust builds, we will have the courage to give honest feedback to one another about the "hidden" areas. As a result, both the hidden areas and the secret areas of our lives will get smaller and the open parts of us increase (see Figure 13). This process can take place in any deep friendship and is an essential part of a marriage relationship if the couple wish to grow in intimacy. In the process, I will understand myself better and become much

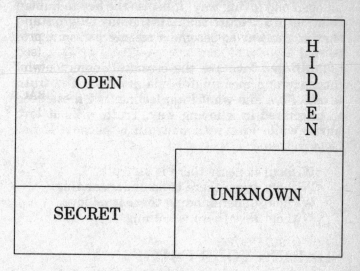

**Figure 13.** Growth in Openness and Self-Esteem

more aware of who I am. It is even possible to get in touch with some of my "unknown" areas. As I learn to accept myself and to be myself, so I will become a more open person and grow in my self-esteem.

This process is only partial here on earth, but we can look forward to the day when it will be complete. "Now we see but a poor reflection . . . then we shall see face to face. Now I know in part; then I shall know fully, even as I am fully known."[7]

*The key to dialogue*

The key to dialogue and true intimacy in relationships is summarised by St Paul: "Speaking the truth in love, we will in all things grow up into him who is the Head, that is, Christ."[8] This is also the basis of a true relationship with God, as we share with him in an open and loving way. It is also the key to human relationships. Notice that it is the way to *"grow up"*, that is, the way to become a mature person and to be real.

Truth and love are the essential ingredients of intimacy and meaningful relationships. The truth is *who I am* and what I am feeling, but these need to be shared in a loving way. Truth without love hurts, while love without truth is phoney. It has been well said:

> Without honesty there is no truth.
> Without truth there is no understanding.
> Without understanding there is no love.
> Without love there is nothing.

## SHARING YOUR FAITH

If you are a Christian, an important part of who you are is being a child of God, not only by creation but by redemption.[9] "A result to be expected from developing a healthy self-esteem as a Christian is the desire to become part of God's redemptive plan."[10] In fact, anyone who is truly overwhelmed by the wonder of being the object of God's amazing love would not be able to keep silent about it! The more we realise our value to God, the more we will be aware of the value of others to him. In the last chapter we stressed the importance of celebrating our uniqueness. There is no one in the world just like you, which means that no one else can glorify God in the way you can. And God has given each one of us a unique job to do.[11]

Unfortunately, many Christians do have a poor self-esteem. Because they find it very difficult to reveal who they are, they lack confidence to share their faith, or may only do so out of guilt or duty. There is a conflict between knowing in their heads that they are loved by God and yet not feeling it in their hearts. A healthy self-esteem is one of the essential factors in becoming a bold ambassador for Christ.

# SUMMARY

Revealing myself, dropping my masks and coming out of my castle takes *courage*. It is not appropriate to do this to everyone or on every occasion, but it is the means by which two human beings develop intimacy. As I share who I am so I discover who I am. When I can accept who I am and be who I am, I will be better able to respect and love myself and to grow in my self-esteem. With a strong self-esteem I will be better equipped to be an authentic witness to my faith.

# REFLECTIONS AND EXERCISES

Begin the first two exercises on your own, recording your thoughts in your journal. To get the most out of these two exercises, share your answers in a group of people who know you and care about you and can give you some honest feed-back.

1 MASKS Can you identify with any of the masks worn by Successful Steven, Sally Super-mum, Marion Martyr, Charlie Cool or Ruth Rescuer? Your mask will not be identical but perhaps a variant of one of these. If none of these masks fit or seem familar to you, try to work out the mask you do wear, especially when you are under pressure or are not feeling good about yourself. If you have difficulty in seeing your mask clearly, ask a close friend to help. Your partner or your children will usually have no problem describing it!

When you have identified your masks clearly, ask yourself these questions.

> Why do I wear this mask?
> Under what situations am I more likely to wear it?
> What encourages me to take it off?
> Does wearing this mask solve my problems?
> Do I want to stop wearing this mask?

CASTLES. We all live in castles of one kind or another. Ask yourself some questions about your "safe retreat":

> How much time do I spend in my castle?
> What makes it difficult for me to come outside my castle?

To whom do I or would I lower my "draw-bridge"?

How often do I in fact do this?

Would I like to come out of my castle more often and really meet others?

What would encourage me to do this?

How and when am I going to begin to do this?

3 DIALOGUE. Do you have someone with whom you can enter into regular dialogue? If you would like this, seek out a friend and share what you want to do. Ask God to help you find the right person. You may be married but have never shared at the level of your feelings for a long time, or perhaps have given up. Why not start now? Set down some goals and "ground-rules". Both of you need to be serious about your desire to grow in self-awareness and openness, and to help each other in this process. Commit yourselves to at least these four values:

| | |
|---|---|
| *Honesty.* | Helping each other have a clear assessment of your own life by being honest with one another. |
| *Confidentiality.* | Agree that nothing shared together will be passed on to another person without permission. |
| *Commitment.* | Determine to grow and to help each other grow. |
| *Accountability.* | Be willing to face up to any issues that may arise and to challenge each other to keep working on them. |

A way to start would be to each talk about yourself, using the dialogue process described earlier, in the following areas:

Your "labels".                              (See Chapter 2)
Your behaviours.                            (See Chapter 4)
Your distorted messages or "tapes".         (See Chapter 6)
Things you dislike about yourself.          (See Chapter 8)
Times you react and do not act.             (See Chapter 9)
Your qualities, gifts and achievements.     (See Chapter 9)
Your masks.                                 (See Chapter 10)
Your feelings.                              (See Chapter 10)

4 To help you be in touch with your feelings, re-run
   a "video" of the past twenty-four hours in your
   mind. Write down all the feelings that you can
   remember having experienced in that time, such
   as: frustration, excitement, disappointment, relief,
   anger or love towards someone.

   ● Make a list of these feelings in one column.
     Then write alongside each one whether you
     shared it with someone or kept it to yourself.
     It may have been appropriate to keep some
     of these feeling to yourself. But were there
     other times when it would have been helpful
     to you or to a relationship if you had shared
     that feeling?
   ● Discuss this experience in your group or with
     a friend or your partner.

5 Refer to the lists of your qualities, gifts and
   achievements (see exercise 1 at the end of the last
   chapter). If you have not done that exercise yet, do
   it now. When you have a number of entries under
   each heading, share them with your "dialogue
   partner", who can reflect back to you his or her
   opinion about what you have written. You may
   now be able to add a lot more items to your list
   which you overlooked before.

- This process can be a valuable tool to help each other understand and evaluate yourselves.
- Use these lists as the basis for praying together. Thank God for all he has given you and done for you, and ask him to develop these qualities, gifts and achievements. Commit yourselves to developing these qualities, gifts or skills with the goal of becoming a more loving person.

# CONCLUSION

Learning to grow in our self-esteem is a challenge. Each of us has been hurt and damaged in various ways in our childhood, often through the ignorance of well-intentioned people or circumstances outside of our control. We have also made wrong choices which could affect us for the rest of our lives. God's image in us has been marred by sin, but it has not been lost. *Jesus came to make people whole* again. God's plan for us is to become the people he created us to be, and this presents us with a worthwhile goal for living. The only thing we all take with us when we die is the person we have become.

When we come to Christ and receive new life, our past is forgiven. "If anyone is in Christ, he is a new creation; the old has gone, the new has come!"[1] God, the "Master Potter", is able to remake us.[2] However, the consequences of our past and the behaviour patterns that we have developed are not immediately changed. The process of sanctification has just begun, but we can grow in grace through the operation of the Holy Spirit in our lives.

Human parents would not want their children to remain as infants, however delightful they might seem at that stage. Also, to insist on doing everything for our children would result in their arrested growth. In the same way, God does not do all the work for us in our journey to wholeness. To do so would keep us immature. Our growth in self-esteem involves our participation as well as the operation of God's grace.

This book has attempted to identify the problem of low self-esteem and how this can inhibit us in our lives and our relationships. We cannot change what we are unaware of, so considerable space has been given to examining good and poor self-esteem and how our self-worth develops. Practical ways have been described in which we can examine our lives, with God's help,[3] and make positive changes towards maturity.

The starting point is *taking responsibility* for ourselves. As we learn to accept and love ourselves, so we can be ourselves and reveal who we are to others. These are components of good self-esteem. A person with good self-esteem will think in a positive cycle (figure 14), which is the reverse of the destructive cycle described in Chapter 2, (figure 1).

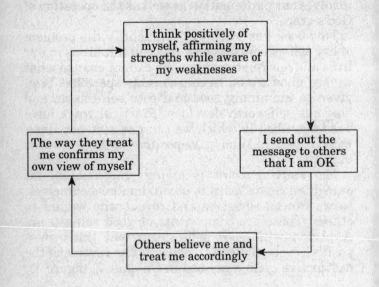

**Figure 14.** The Positive Self-Esteem Cycle

# CREATED FOR LOVE

We have all been created to be loved and to love. Our prayer is that this book will help you in your journey towards becoming a more loving person: loving yourself and others unconditionally, and loving God more fully.

# REFERENCES AND NOTES

## INTRODUCTION

1) Henry Thoreau, philosopher, poet and essayist, 1817–1862.
2) This was certainly St Paul's goal in life. See Philippians 3:7–11.
3) Carl Sandburg.
4) Lawrence Osborne, *Paper Pilgrimage* (London, Daybreak, 1990) pp 2–3.
5) 1 John 4:19. The AV translation of this verse is often quoted, "We love him because he first loved us". This of course, is true, but in the original Greek text the word "him" is not present. What John is saying is that we are only able to love at all, God or people, in response to God's love for us.
6) John 10:10.
7) John 8:32.
8) See Romans 5:3,4; James 1:2–4.

## CHAPTER 1

1) Proverbs 23:7 (Authorised Version).
2) Philippians 1:6.
3) Romans 12:3.
4) The difference between true and false guilt is discussed in Chapter 4.
5) For an excellent introduction to the importance and value of solitude and silence see:
*The Way of the Heart* by Henri Nouwen (London, Daybreak, 1981).
*Space for God* by David Runcorn (London, Daybreak, 1990).

*Celebration of Discipline* by Richard Foster (London, Hodder and Stoughton, Revised Edition, 1989), Chapter 7.

6) Eugene Kennedy, *If You Really Knew Me, Would You Still Love Me* (Illinois, Argus Communications, 1975), p 33.

7) *The Talmud.*

8) Leviticus 19:18; Matthew 19:19; 22:39; Mark 12:31; Luke 10:27; Romans 13:9; Galatians 5:14; Ephesians 5:28, 33; James 2:8.

9) A term coined by the psychologist Eric Erikson. See John & Paula Sandford's excellent statement on building basic trust in children; *Restoring the Christian Family* (U.K., Bridge Publishing, 1984) p 4 ff. Refer also to Chapter 3 in this book.

10) Philippians 2:4.

11) John Powell, *Why I Am Afraid to Tell You Who I Am.* (Illinois, Argus, 1969).

12) An excellent book that explores this is by Dennis and Barbara Rainey, *Building Your Mate's Self-Esteem* (San Bernadino, Here's Life Publishers, 1986).

13) Genesis 4:3–9.

14) Proverbs 14:30.

15) This phrase "fully human and fully alive" comes from a book of that same title by John Powell, (Illinois, Argus, 1976).

16) Genesis 1:27; James 3:9.

17) Francis Schaeffer, *Genesis in Space and Time* (Downers Grove, Illinois, Inter-Varsity, 1972) pp 46, 51–52.

18) Ephesians 2:10.

19) Romans 12:2.

20) This test is an adaptation of one designed by M.H. Kuhn as a measure of self-concept. In that test, people were requested to write down 20 answers to the question: "Who am I?" as quickly as possible. The results were analysed and found to reveal a lot of information about people's attitudes to themselves and to others. Reference: Kuhn and McPortland, "An Empirical Investigation of Self-Attitudes" (*American Social Review*, 19th Feb 1954) pp 68–76.

# CHAPTER 2

1) This is one reason why people find it so hard to grasp that salvation cannot be earned, but has to be received by faith. See Romans 4:1–8; Galatians 3:10–14; Ephesians 2:8–9.
2) Eric Berne described the beliefs and prejudices that are part of our "Parent" ego state, as "taped messages", in his Transactional Analysis Theory of personality.
3) Victor Frankl, *The Doctor and the Soul* (New York, Alfred A. Knopf, Inc., 1965).
4) Albert Ellis, *The Case Against Religiosity* (New York, Institute for Rational-Emotive Therapy, 1983).
5) We are indebted to Mrs Margaret Mourant, Auckland, New Zealand, for some of the ideas in this section.
6) A comprehensive book describing ways of dealing with cognitive distortions is *Self Esteem* by M. McKay and P. Flemming (Oakland, CA, New Harbinger Publications, 1987) Chapters 5 and 7.
7) Low self-esteem is the soil in which loneliness often develops, especially for teenagers. (See Chapter 4.)
8) Charles Whitfield, *Healing the Child Within* (Dearfield, Fl., Health Communications, Inc, 1987) Chapter 6.
9) THE SCORE OF YOUR TEST. If you have scored a total of 60 or more, it means that the self-esteem issue is something you should be working on. This book is designed to show how to do this. After working through the book, we suggest that you repeat this exercise. You may be surprised how much you have changed.

# CHAPTER 3

1) Proverbs 22:6 (The Living Bible).
2) Thomas Verny, *The Secret Life of the Unborn Child* (London, Sphere Books Ltd., 1982) page x.
3) D.H. Scott, "Children of the Womb: The Effects of Stress", *New Society*, pp 329–331, May 19, 1977.
4) D.H. Scott, "Follow-Up Study from Birth of the Effects of Pre-Natal Stress", *Develop. Med. Child. Neurol.*, 15 (1973) pp 770–787.

5) Frank Lake, *Tight Corners in Pastoral Counselling* (London, Darton, Longman & Todd, 1981).

6) M.Lukesch, *Z-Klin-Psychol-Psychother und Zeitschrift fur Klinische Psychologie und Psychotherapie*, 1978, Vol. 26, No. 4. pp 348–365.

7) Verny, op. cit., page xi.

8) Luke 1:36–44.

9) Luke 1:56.

10) Matthew & Dennis Linn, *Healing the Eight Stages of Life* (New York, Paulist Press, 1991).

11) Erik H. Erikson, *Childhood and Society* (St Albans, Triad Paladin, U.K., 1977) p 222.

12) J. Stone and J. Church, *Childhood and Adolescence*, 3rd Edition (New York, Random House, 1973) p 492.

13) The effects of interruption to the love process (or loss of attachment) on young children is well documented by British psychiatrist John Bowlby in his book, *Attachment and Loss* (London, Hogarth Press, 1969–82).

14) C.S. Lewis, *The Four Loves* (London, Geoffrey Bles Ltd, 1960).

15) Ross Campbell, *How to Really Love Your Teenager* (Wheaton, Illinois, Victor Books, 1982) p 25.

16) John Powell, *Unconditional Love* (Illinois, Argus Communications, 1978) p 70.

17) Erich Fromm, *The Art of Loving* (London, Unwin paperback, 1975) p 38.

18) Campbell, op. cit., p 15. Chapter 4 explores ways of expressing focused attention to teenagers.

19) Dr Wilson Grant has written an excellent book, *The Power of Affirming Touch* (Minneapolis, Augsburg Publishing House, 1986) in which he elaborates on the value of eye contact.

20) Matthew 6:22.

21) These statements on the importance of eye contact are made in the context of European culture, and would possibly hold true for all cultures in the family or close relationships. However, in some Pacific Island cultures, such as Samoan, it is disrespectful to look an older person or someone of superior rank in the eye. In many Asian cultures, looking someone in the eye in public is not done.

22) Ashley Montague, *Touching* (New York, Harper & Row, 1971) p 4.

23) Sidney Simon, *Caring, Feeling, Touching* (Niles, Illinois, 1976).

24) Ashley Montague, op. cit., p 2: cites research showing that the human embryo of about six weeks will respond to touch.

25) References 22, 23 & 24 will provide extensive information on the significance of touch and the research that has been done.

26) Jules Older, *Touching is Healing* (New York, Stein and Day, 1982) p 48.

27) David Seamands, "Affirm the Present Achievement", article in *Parents and Children* (Wheaton, Illinois, Victoria Books, 1986).

28) Erich Fromm, op. cit.

29) Baars and Terruwe, *Healing the Unaffirmed* (1972).

30) M Scott Peck, *The Road Less Travelled* (London, Century Hutchinson, 1985) p 24.

31) Ephesians 4:22–23.

32) *Mister God This Is Anna*, by Fynn (London, Collins, 1974).

# CHAPTER 4

1) Matthew 13:12.

2) John Donne (1571–1631), *Devotions XVII*.

3) Genesis 2:18.

4) Genesis 1:26.

5) See Paul's argument in Romans chapter 14.

6) Wayne Oates, *Confessions of a Workaholic* (Nashville, Abingdon, 1971) p 5.

7) Examples of biblical teaching on the dignity and value of work: Genesis 2:15; Proverbs 6:6–11; 18:9; 31:10–29; Ephesians 4:28; 1 Thessalonians 1:3; 4:11; 2 Thessalonians 3:6–13; 2 Timothy 2:15.

8) Galatians 1:10 and 2 Corinthians 5:9 (The Living Bible).

9) Sigmund Freud, *The Defence Neuro-Psychoses* (1894) and *Inhibitions, Symptoms and Anxiety* (1926).

10) Charles Morris, *Psychology, An Introduction* (New Jersey, Prentice Hall), p 439.

11) Two useful outlines of common defence mechanisms and some Christian alternatives are:

    a) Paul Meier, et al., *Introduction to Psychology & Counselling: Christian Perspectives & Applications* (Grand Rapids, Baker Book House, 1982) Chapter 18.

    b) Quentin Hyder, *The People You Live With* (New Jersey, Flemming H. Revell Company, 1975) Chapter 3.

12) John Powell, *Fully Human, Fully Alive* (Valencia, CA, Tabor Publishing, 1976).

13) Gary Collins, *Overcoming Anxiety* (Santa Anna, Vision House, 1973) pp 82–83.

14) The original fairy story was written by the brothers Grimm early in the 19th century, and later adapted by Walt Disney (at which time the dwarfs were given their names).

15) John 1:14 (The Living Bible).

16) Aaron T. Beck et al., *Cognitive Therapy of Depression* (New York, The Guilford Press, 1979).

17) Janice Wood Wetzel, *Clinical Handbook of Depression* (New York, Gardner Press, 1984) pp 17–67.

18) James Dobson, *Man to Man About Women* (London, Coverdale House Ltd., 1975) p 22.

19) Paul Tournier, *Guilt and Grace* (New York, Harper & Row, 1962) p 64.

20) Ibid., pp 64–70.

21) 1 John 1:9.

22) Romans 12:2.

23) Leslie Carter, Paul Meier, Frank Minirth, *Why Be Lonely* (Grand Rapids, Baker Book House, 1982).

24) Abraham Twerski, *Like Yourself and Others Will, Too* (New Jersey, Prentice Hall, 1978).

25) Rubin Zick, "Seeking a Cure for Loneliness", *Psychology Today*, October 1979, pp 82–90.

26) Josh McDowell, *How To Help Your Child Say "No" To Sexual Pressure* (Milton Keynes U.K., Word Publishing) p 67.

27) Jocelyn Roberts, *Self-Image and Delinquency* (New Zealand, Dept. of Justice, 1972).

28) Eric Berne, *Games People Play* (U.K. & U.S.A. Penguin Books,) Chapter 5.

29) Helena Wilkinson, "Self Esteem or Self Efficiency?", *The Christian Counsellor*, Volume 1, No 3, p 40.

30) See Ephesians 4:29; 1 Thessalonians 5:11; Hebrews 10:25.

31) Genesis 3:8–10.

32) Compare Luke 18:10–14 and 20:47. The Pharisee in the temple was so used to wearing a mask before people that he even kept it on before God.

33) Matthew 13:12.

34) Proverbs 9:9.

35) There is no pass or fail score. The higher your score out of 60, the better your self-esteem.


# CHAPTER 5


1) Josh McDowell, *His Image, My Image* (Amersham-on-the-Hill, UK, Scripture Press Foundation, 1985) p 34.

2) Thomas à Kempis, *The Imitation of Christ* (Glasgow, Collins, Fount Paperbacks, 1977). Translated from the Latin by Betty Knott. Extracts from Book I (2); Book 3 (8) and (40).

3) John Calvin, *Institutes of the Christian Religion* (Philadelphia, Presbyterian Board of Christian Education, 1928, translated by J.Albau) p 622.

4) Roy Hession, *The Calvary Road* (Fort Washington, PA., Christian Literature Crusade, 1964) p 15.

5) Psalm 22:6.

6) Job 25:6.

7) Job 42:7.

8) Psalm 8:5,6. Compare with Genesis 1:26–28. See also Hebrews 2:6–8.

9) Psalm 82:6.

10) John 10:34–35.

11) Francis Schaeffer, *Genesis in Time and Space* (Illinois, Inter Varsity Press, 1972) p 50.

12) A.H. Strong, *Systematic Theology* (Old Tappan, N.J., Flemming H. Revell, 1907) p 110.

13) Matthew 13:45–46. This parable has a double interpretation. The usual interpretation is a person discovering Christ, "the Pearl of great price" and selling all for him.

But seen from heaven's perspective, it is a picture of Christ selling all in order to purchase the "pearl", the Church. See Campbell Morgan, *The Parables and Metaphors of Jesus* (London, Marshall, Morgan & Scott, 1943) pp 62–67.

14) Deuteronomy 7:7–8.

15) Romans 5:8.

16) See *You're Someone Special* by Bruce Narramore (Grand Rapids, Zondervan, 1978) for an excellent discussion of this issue, in Chapter 4.

17) See *Theological Dictionary of the New Testament*, ed. Gerhard Kittel, Trans. Geoffrey Bromily, vol 2. (Grand Rapids, Eerdmans, 1964) for a thorough treatment of the use of the word "ego" in the New Testament.

18) John 12:32.

19) W.E.Vine, *Expository Dictionary of New Testament Words* (New Jersey, Flemming H. Revell, 1946) p 341.

20) 1 Peter 2:24.

21) Matthew 19:5.

22) W.E. Vine, op. cit. pp 107–108.

23) Romans 7:18.

24) 1 Corinthians 9:24–27.

25) 1 Corinthians 6:19.

26) Romans 12:1.

27) Romans 8:5–13.

28) Romans 8:8; Galatians 5:19–21.

29) Ephesians 4:13. See also, Romans 8:29; 2 Corinthians 3:18.

30) *Universal Dictionary* (Reader's Digest, London, 1988).

31) Josh McDowell, *His Image, My Image* (Amersham-on-the-Hill, Bucks, Scripture Press Foundation, 1985) p 34.

32) Genesis 1:27; 1 Corinthians 11:7b; James 3:9.

33) 2 Corinthians 4:4; Colossians 1:15; Hebrews 1:3.

34) Genesis 1:26.

35) For a superb introduction to the wonder of the human mind see Gary Collins, *Your Magnificent Mind* (Grand Rapids, Baker, 1985).

36) Some examples of this: Deuteronomy 30:19–20; Joshua 24:15; Acts 2:21; Revelation 22:17.

37) Song of Songs 8:6–7; John 15:13.

38) Bruce Narramore: op. cit. p 38.

39) We acknowledge assistance with some of these facts from

a book by Dr Paul Brand and Philip Yancey, *In His Image* (London, Hodder and Stoughton, 1984).

40) Psalm 139:14 (Jerusalem Bible)
41) Jeremiah 31:3.
42) 1 John 3:1.
43) Isaiah 64:4; 1 Corinthians 2:9.
44) John 17:23.
45) John 15:9.
46) Romans 5:5 (The Living Bible). See also Ephesians 3:16–19.
47) Luke 15:31.
48) Psalm 139:15–16. See also Jeremiah 1:5; Galatians 1:15.
49) Psalm 139:2–5 (The Living Bible).
50) Isaiah 43:1; 49:16.
51) John 10:3.
52) Matthew 10:30.
53) Zechariah 2:8. See also Deuteronomy 32:10; Psalm 17:8.
54) See Eugene Nida, *Religion Across Culture* (New York, Harper & Row, 1968) pp 80–83.
55) Galatians 2:20.
56) Bruce Narramore, op. cit. p 137.
57) Ephesians 1:6 (Authorised Version).
58) Acts 10:34,35.
59) Romans 15:7.
60) Psalm 116:1; 1 John 5:14. Other examples: Psalm 34:6, 17. Isaiah 65:24; Jeremiah 29:12; Matthew 7:7.
61) Isaiah 1:18; 43:26.
62) Abraham – Genesis chapter 18; Moses – Exodus chapters 33, 34; Job – chapters 38–40; Nicodemus – John 3:1–21; Samaritan woman – John 4:4–26.
63) Exodus 33:11; Isaiah 41:8; James 2:23.
64) Romans 5:10 (Good News Bible). See also Colossians 1:21,22.
65) Romans 8:15,23; Galatians 4:5 (AV); Ephesians 1:5.
66) Galatians 4:4–7.
67) Ephesians 2:19 (The Living Bible).
68) Ephesians 3:17–19 (The Living Bible).
69) Colossians 1:15 (Good News Bible).
70) Matthew 9:10–13; 11:19; Luke 5:27–32; 15:1–2.
71) John 4:1–42.
72) Luke 19:1–10.
73) John 3:17.
74) John 8:1–11.
75) Luke 7:36–50. The word "woman" (verse 44) is the same

word Jesus used to address his mother: 'gune'. (See John 2:4; 19:26.)

76) A.H. Strong: op. cit. page 103.

77) Ephesians 1:11,18. (The Living Bible). See also Deuteronomy 7:6; Malachi 3:17.

78) Matthew 22:37,38.

79) Leviticus 19:18.

80) Romans 13:9; Galatians 5:14; Ephesians 5:28,33; James 2:8.

81) Romans 7:15,24.

82) Revelation 12:10.

83) Romans 8:1,2.

84) 2 Timothy 3:2–4.

85) Galatians 5:13–14.

86) *Meister Eckhart*. Translated by R.B. Blakeney (London, Watkins, 1955).

87) Philippians 2:3 (Authorised Version).

88) Luke 22:24.

89) Matthew 16:24–25.

90) William Barclay, *The Gospel of Matthew, Vol. 2* (Edinburgh, The Saint Andrew Press, 1958) p 168.

91) M. Scott Peck, *The Road Less Travelled* (London, Century Hutchinson, 1985) p 72.

92) Ephesians 1:4–6.

93) Luke 18:29–30.

94) John 10:10.

95) Joanna and Alister McGrath, *The Dilemma of Self-Esteem* (Cambridge, England, Crossway Books, 1992) p 123.

96) Morton Kelsey, *Caring: How Can We Love One Another?* (New York, Paulist Press, 1981) p 58.

97) Romans 15:7

# CHAPTER 6

1) Deuteronomy 30:19.

2) M. Scott Peck, *The Road Less Travelled* (London, Century Hutchinson, 1983) p 64.

3) John White, *Changing on the Inside* (Guildford, Surrey, Eagle, 1991) p 50.

4) John Powell, *Fully Human, Fully Alive* (Valencia, California, Tabor Publishing, 1976) p 79.
5) The "drama triangle", or Karpman Triangle, is a concept describing the way people often interact in the following roles, and frequently change roles:

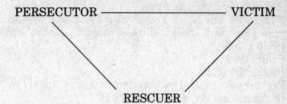

PERSECUTOR ——————————— VICTIM

RESCUER

Persecutor, Victim Rescuer a/w here

This concept was first described by Stephen Karpman in "Fairy Tale and Script Drama Analysis", *Transactional Analysis Bulletin 36* (April 1968) pp 35–43.
6) See Ephesians 4:15. This the key to close relationships: "Speaking the truth in love."
7) Genesis 3:12.
8) 2 Samuel 12:1–14.
9) Plato (428–348 BC): *Dialogues*.
10) Hebrews 4:12.
11) For an expansion of these areas of our vision see John Powell, op. cit., especially Chapter 4. Also, the "Fully Alive Experience", by John Powell and Loretta Brady is an excellent cassette tape course about examining and changing our vision.
12) Epictetus, *The Encheiridion*.
13) 1 Corinthians 13:11.
14) 2 Corinthians 10:4–5.
15) Galatians 1:10 (The Living Bible).
16) Thomas à Kempis, *The Imitation of Christ*, translated by William Creasy (Macon, GA, Mercer University Press, 1989) p 23.
17) 1 Thessalonians 5:11.
18) Alice and Walden Howard, *Exploring The Road Less Travelled* (London Arrow Books, 1988) p 28.
19) Dorothy Corkill Briggs, *Your Child's Self Esteem* (New York, Dolphin Books, Doubleday, 1975) p 43.

# CHAPTER 7

1) Narcissus was a youth from Greek mythology, who, having spurned the love of Echo, fell in love with his own reflection in a pool of water and was transformed into a flower, the narcissus.

2) Eugene Kennedy, *If You Really Knew Me, Would You Still Love Me?* (Niles, Illinois, Argus Communications, 1975) p 105.

3) Psalm 26:2.

4) Psalm 139:23,24.

5) Proverbs 20:24,27. See also: Deuteronomy 8:2.

6) St Augustine, *Confessions, Book 10.*

7) Richard Foster, *Prayer: Finding the Heart's True Home* (London, Hodder & Stoughton, 1992) p 32.

8) Paul Tournier, *The Meaning of Persons* (London, SCM Press, 1970).

9) Ibid., p 15.

10) Romans 12:15 (Authorised Version; Good News Bible).

11) J.L. Marino has written extensively on the many and varied roles we all play throughout life, and has used this understanding in the development of his Psycho-Drama Therapy.

12) Bruce Narramore, *You're Someone Special* (Grand Rapids, Zondervan Publishing House, 1978) p 151.

13) John 1:14 (The Living Bible).

14) Margery Williams, *The Velveteen Rabbit* (Philadelphia, Running Press, 1984).

15) Matthew 7:1. See also Romans 14:4,10.

16) 1 Corinthians 4:3–5.

17) 1 Corinthians 2:15; 1 Thessalonians 5:21; 1 John 4:1.

18) Romans 12:3.

19) Genesis 6:5 (AV). See also Genesis 8:21 and Deuteronomy 31:21.

20) 1 Chronicles 28:9; 29:18 (Authorised Version).

21) Isaiah 26:3.

22) Leslie D. Weatherhead, *Prescription for Anxiety* (New York, Abingdon Press,).

23) 1 Corinthians 9:24.

24) Psalm 23:1.

25) John 10:3.

26) Matthew 13:10–13

27) See Ephesians 4:15.
28) The concept of taking a personal inventory comes from the 12-Step Programme, used so effectively by Alcoholics Anonymous. This has helped many thousands of alcoholics to make life-saving changes. The Fourth step is one of the most important: "Make a searching and fearless moral inventory of ourselves" followed up by the 10th step: "Continue to take a personal inventory, and when we are wrong, promptly admit it." For further information, see: *Alcoholics Anonymous* (New York, Alcoholics Anonymous World Service, Inc., originally published in 1939).
29) For further examples of picturing and meditating see:
    a) *The Smile of Love* by Joyce Huggett (Sevenoaks, Kent, Hodder & Stoughton, 1990) pp 53–77.
    b) *The Other Side of Silence* by Morton Kelsey (New York, Paulist Press, 1976) pp 208–308.
30) This exercise was designed by John Powell and Loretta Brady in their "Fully Alive Experience" course.

# CHAPTER 8

1) Matthew 22:39.
2) Joyce Huggett, *Living Free – Becoming the Person God Intends You To Be* (Leicester, Inter-Varsity Press, 1984) p 109.
3) Romans 15:7. See also Acts 10:35.
4) Ephesians 1:6 (AV).
5) Josh McDowell, *His Image, My Image* (Amersham-on-the-Hill, Scripture Press Foundation, U.K. Ltd., 1985) pp 151–152.
6) Maurice Wagner, *The Sensation of Being Somebody* (New York, Harper Paperback, 1991) p 29.
7) Joanna and Alister McGrath, *The Dilemma of Self Esteem* (Wheaton, Illinois, Crossways Books, 1992) p 33.
8) Matthew 28:20; Hebrews 13:5.
9) Malachi 3:17; John 10:14; 1 Corinthians 6:19, 20.
10) Romans 8:28, 39.
11) See Psalm 8:3–5; 139:14–16.
12) Used with permission, *Grapevine* magazine, July 1989 (Auckland, NZ).

13) James 3:5–12.
14) Romans 12:3.
15) Dick Wulf, *Find Yourself, Give Yourself* (Colorado Springs, Navpress, 1983) p 129.
16) 2 Corinthians 12:9–10.
17) Reinhold Niebuhr.
18) Philippians 4:11–12.
19) Hebrews 12:15.
20) Matthew 6:12–15.
21) Matthew 18:22.
22) Jeremiah 31:34. See also Psalm 103:12; Micah 7:19.
23) Luke 23:34.
24) Luke 6:37.
25) John 13:34.
26) 1 Samuel 20:17.
27) Supplied by Rev Gordon Hambly, Auckland, New Zealand.
28) Romans 12:3 (The Living Bible).

# CHAPTER 9

1) William Shakespeare, *Hamlet*, Act I, Scene III, speech by Polonius to Laertes.
2) Ephesians 4:13; Colossians 1:28. See also 2 Corinthians 3:18.
3) See 1 Corinthians 4:16; 11:1; 1 Thessalonians 1:6–7.
4) Josh McDowell, *His Image, My Image* (Amersham-on-the-Hill, U.K., Scripture Press, 1988) p 9.
5) James Masterson, *The Search for the Real Self* (New York, The Free Press, Macmillan, 1988) p 29.
6) Maurice Wagner, *The Sensation of Being Somebody* (New York, Harper Paperbacks, 1991) p 56.
7) Genesis 2:24.
8) This is an effective exercise in dealing with unresolved issues relating to someone who has died, or who is not available for discussion. It is known as the "two-chair" process, where you sit in one chair and place the other person in the other chair, in your imagination. It is possible in this way to "talk" to that person and resolve hurts from the past.
9) Philippians 1:10 (Authorised Version).

10) Ephesians 2:10b.
11) John Powell, *Happiness Is An Inside Job* (Allen, Texas, Tabor Publishing, 1989) p 21.
12) Gifts of the Spirit: See Romans 12:6–8; 1 Corinthians 12:1–11.
13) Galatians 5:22, 23.
14) 1 Corinthians 13:1–3.
15) Ephesians 3:17 (The Living Bible).
16) Ephesians 4:15. (Revised Standard Version).
17) Matthew 3:17.
18) Friedrich Nietzsche, German classical scholar and philosopher, Professor of Classical Philology, University of Basel 1869–79.
19) 1 John 2:16.
20) See 1 Peter 2:23.
21) 1 Corinthians 4:12–13.
22) Henri J.M. Nouwen, *!Gracias!* (San Francisco, Harper & Row, 1982) p 30.
23) Philippians 4:13.
24) Robert Bolton, *People Skills* (New Jersey, Prentice-Hall, Inc, 1979) p 125. This is an excellent book on how to learn good assertiveness skills.
25) See Matthew chapter 23 and John chapter 8.
26) John 18:23.
27) James and Jongeward, *Born To Win* (Reading, Massachusetts, Addison-Wesley Publishing Company 1977) p 1.
28) Sydney Harris, *Winners and Losers* (Niles, Illinois, Argus Communications, 1973). Items marked "H" are from this book and those marked "B" are from *Born To Win*.
29) Luke 2:52.
30) Matthew 5:23–24; 1 John 4:19.
31) Martin Buber, *I and Thou* (Edinburgh. T & T Clark, 1966).
32) Paul Tillich, *The Courage to Be* (Collins, Fount Paperbacks, 1980) p 183.
33) Suggested changes in exercise 5:

"I don't feel understood."
"I am angry."
"I don't feel heard."
"I don't believe that."
"I'm lonely."

"I find it hard to be myself around here."

"Please help me."

"I like being with you."

"I'm scared when you drive so fast."

"I love you, Lord. Please help me to love you more."

# CHAPTER 10

1) 1 John 4:19.

2) Hebrews 1:1–2.

3) Paul Tournier, *The Meaning of Persons* (London, SCM Press, 1970).

4) Bruce Narramore, *You're Someone Special* (Grand Rapids, Zondervan, 1978) p 167.

5) Joseph Loft, *Group Processes: An Introduction to Group Dynamics* (National Press Books, 1963).

6) See Psalm 51:6,10; 139:23; Ephesians 4:22.

7) 1 Corinthians 13:12.

8) Ephesians 4:15.

9) 1 John 3:1.

10) Josh McDowell, *His Image, My Image* (Amersham-on-the Hill, U.K., Scripture Press, 1984) p 168.

11) Ephesians 2:10. See also the following examples of the way God calls individuals to specific tasks from before birth, even before conception: Jeremiah 1:5; Luke 1:13–17; Galatians 1:15–16.

# CONCLUSION

1) 2 Corinthians 5:17.

2) Jeremiah 18:1–5.

3) Psalm 139:23–24.

# SELECTED BIBLIOGRAPHY

This is a brief reading guide to some significant books dealing with the issues we have
addressed. It reflects our personal bias, namely that
we base what we believe and have written on the
word of God and on proven insights of psychology
and medicine.

*You're Someone Special* by Bruce Narramore (Grand
Rapids, Michigan, Zondervan Publishing House,
1978).

A penetrating analysis of the concept of self-
acceptance and learning how to love yourself in a
healthy way. As Professor of Psychology at a Christian College, Dr Narramore combines a psychological
understanding of human personality with a sound
biblical perspective to give a balanced picture of what
is a good self-concept.

*The Art of Learning to Love Yourself* by Cecil Osborne
(Grand Rapids, Zondervan, 1976).

This book is a thoughtful description of what a
weak self-image is like and also how to grow in
healthy self-love. Dr Osborne illustrates the text
with many stories drawn from his considerable
experience as a pastor and psychotherapist. He
explains the value of properly run, small sharing
groups for helping people grow in their identity and

self-worth. This concept is developed in greater detail in his companion volume: *The Art of Understanding Yourself* (Zondervan, 1967).

*His Image, My Image* by Josh McDowell (Amersham-on-the Hill, England, Scripture Press, 1985).

An easy-to-read book which defines the problem of a low self-image and also what a good self-image should be like. The author outlines positive steps that can be taken to build a good self-esteem in line with a sound biblical understanding of this concept. At the end of each chapter are some brief exercises to work on. The book would appeal to thinking young people.

*Building Your Mate's Self-Esteem* by Dennis & Barbara Rainey (San Bernadino, CA., Here's Life Publishers, 1986).

Dr James Dobson said: "The most successful marriages are those where both husband and wife seek to build the self-esteem of each other." This excellent book sets out to show how this can be done, drawing on sound psychological, biblical and practical principles. Each chapter has brief exercises to work through.

*How to Really Love Your Child. / How to Really Love Your Teenager* by Ross Campbell (Wheaton, Victor, SP Publications, 1977, 1981).

These two books describe how to demonstrate unconditional love to your children effectively through eye contact, touch, focused attention, loving discipline and spiritual encouragement. These are the same principles required to build a child's self-esteem. As a psychiatrist, Dr Campbell combines sound psychological understanding with strong Christian faith.

*Hide or Seek* by James Dobson (New Jersey, Flemming H. Revell Co., 1974).

This is now a classic book describing effective ways to build a child's self-esteem and sense of personal worth. An experienced psychologist and committed Christian, Dr Dobson outlines strategies which will encourage the development of healthy self-esteem in early years, middle childhood, adolescence and as adults. He offers practical advice for a number of specific questions and parenting problems.

*Your Child's Self-Esteem* by Dorothy Corkill Briggs (New York, Doubleday, 1970).

This is a very practical and readable book. It is full of accurate information about childhood development and much sensitive wisdom. The author presents step-by-step guidelines for raising responsible, productive and happy children. She addresses very well the relationship between discipline and self-esteem and how to deal effectively with negative feelings.

*52 Simple Ways to Build Your Child's Self-Esteem* by Jan Dargatz (Nashville, Thomas Nelson, 1991).

This book contains 52 short chapters, each with a very practical and sometimes novel way to help children become confident and value themselves. By being prepared for the many different situations they may face, life can be positive and exciting.

*100 Ways to Enhance Self-concept in the Classroom* by Jack Canfield and Harold Wells (New Jersey, Prentice-Hall, 1976).

This book is designed primarily for teachers as a guide to developing the self-esteem of students in the classroom. Naturally, these practical and creative ideas can be adapted and used by parents, or anyone interested in children.

*The Meaning of Persons* by Paul Tournier (London, SCM Press, 1957).

This book comes out of the profound reflections of a deeply committed Christian psychiatrist. Dr Tournier gives a very clear answer to the question "Who am I?" He clarifies the difference between the two parts of a human being: the "Person" (my self of reality) and the "Personage" (my self-picture). An understanding of this helps in the integration of the personality.

*Living Free* by Joyce Huggett (Leicester, Inter-Varsity Press, 1984).

The author explores the meaning of true freedom in terms of "becoming the person God intended you to be". Joyce Huggett describes the process of growth into freedom, spiritually and emotionally. Through sharing the stories of many people, this journey to freedom is made real and understandable in terms of everyday living.

*The Sensation of Being Somebody* by Maurice Wagner (New York, Harper Paperbacks, Collins, 1975).

An experienced Pastor, Dr Wagner combines a biblical and psychological understanding of the development of our self-concept. He explores the significance of the feelings of belonging, worthiness and competence in the formation of our sense of self-worth. He goes on to describe practical ways to grow emotionally and spiritually and overcome self-defeating patterns of behaviour.

*In His Image* by Paul Brand and Philip Yancey (London, Hodder & Stoughton, 1984).

A fascinating and informative book about the marvels of the human body, written by a skilled surgeon and the editor-in-chief of *Christianity Today*. The authors make a helpful bridge from the natural world of the human body to the spiritual world of the Body of Christ. They also offer some powerful insights into the meaning of pain.

*Self-Assertion for Women* by Pamela Butler (San Francisco, Harper, 1981). New Edition.

In this book, Dr Butler, a clinical psychologist, teaches the principles of direct, honest communication. She offers practical advice, realistic examples and step-by-step exercises in how to be healthily assertive without being aggressive. The author elaborates on many skills, including speaking for yourself, using "I" messages; expressing negative feelings effectively and learning how to say "No". She shows how a woman can achieve feminism without losing femininity and how to improve communication in all situations.

*Fully Human, Fully Alive* by John Powell (Valencia, California, Tabor Publishing, 1976).

The author shows how our expectations, feelings and reactions are determined by our "vision" or belief system. Our vision covers five major areas: how we view ourselves, others, life, the world and God. For all of us, our vision has been distorted in some way. John Powell presents helpful ways to challenge and change distorted vision, which he calls Vision Therapy.

*Unconditional Love* by John Powell (Niles, Illinois, Argus Communications, 1978).

John Powell in this challenging book shows the

life principle of learning and practising real love – unconditional love. This kind of love was fully demonstrated in the life of Jesus, a model for us to follow. The author describes how to become a free, whole and loving person, committed to loving others as I love myself.

*The Dilemma of Self-Esteem* by Joanna and Alister McGrath (Cambridge, England, Crossways Books, 1992).

This significant book is written by a psychologist and a theologian. They present an in-depth analysis of modern psychological research and understanding of self-esteem, evaluated from a Christian perspective. They also give a clear theological statement as the basis for a Christian's self-esteem.

# GROWTH GROUPS

The development of self-esteem is a personal issue and something that no one else can do for me. But self-esteem problems are universal and affect everybody. So while I need to do the work of growing in self-esteem myself, it is very helpful to have the support of others in this process. This is why we have suggested in many of the exercises throughout this book that there would be great benefits from sharing your experiences and insights in a small group.

A small growth group can be the vehicle of much healing. It can also provide a lot of support to people who are struggling with difficult or painful issues in their personal lives. However, the group needs to be properly structured for people to derive maximum benefit from it. It is important to ensure that the group is a *safe place* for people to share and grow. Many people have not had experience of small groups and are unaware of how to run a growth group properly. The following are some guidelines which we have found to be essential for the proper functioning of small groups. It would be helpful for people intending to form a growth group to study them. Perhaps they could provide the material for the first group meeting. Sections 6–10 could well be read out in the group from time to time subsequently.

It is important that all participants in a group understand the ground rules and agree to them.

They can even give each other permission to point it out if one member overlooks something that has been agreed upon together.

# SMALL GROUP DYNAMICS

1. **The setting.** A home environment is a good place, providing that it is free from interruptions by children or telephone. It needs to be geographically central for group members. Sometimes varying the location from home to home is helpful. Appointing someone, or a couple to act as "host/hostess" can be helpful, depending on the size of the group and how well people know each other already. In some situations, a neutral venue is better than a home. This should be a group decision.

2. **Size of the group.** The ideal size for a small group is about six to eight people. A smaller group can be quite successful, but people may feel more vulnerable in a group of three or four, unless they already know each other well. On the other hand, with more than eight in a group some people may miss out on opportunities to participate fully. Others may use a larger group as an excuse to hide and so fail to benefit from being involved. It is fine if perhaps a larger group wish to meet together to study the material together, so long as the exercises are done in small groups.

3. **Attendance.** It is important for participants in small groups to make a commitment to attend regularly. When members are missing, it alters the dynamics of the group significantly. Some

people are afraid to commit themselves to anything long-term. A way round this is for the group to agree to meet for say six weeks and then renegotiate for blocks of a few sessions at a time, until the group has run its natural course. This is far better than for the group to disintegrate through attrition.

4. **Frequency of meetings.** One group meeting a week is probably the ideal, although fortnightly will work well. But spacing it more than two weeks apart will make continuity more difficult. Allow about one and a half to two hours for each session. After two hours, energy levels drop off, especially when dealing with fairly emotive topics. Starting and finishing times should be defined clearly and an effort made by everyone to keep faith with these. If some members feel the need to stay longer to talk, they can do so after the group has formally closed.

5. **Leadership.** Small groups need leadership or facilitating in the early stages, especially if members are not used to the process. The job of the facilitator is not to control the meetings, but to ensure that the group process functions properly. As the group develops a life of its own and starts to function well, the leader can take less executive control in order to encourage the development of a leaderless group. This is ideal.

6. **Communication.** The main task of the leader is to facilitate good communication within the group. The important principles of healthy group dynamics are:

a) *Be a good listener.* When one member of the

group is speaking, it is the task of the others to give that person focussed attention and to listen to what she/he is saying. Any comments by others should be directed towards clarification, rather than evaluation, of anything the speaker is saying which may not be clear. Try to put yourself in the speaker's shoes; try to feel what it is like to be them. Live their experiences with them. When she/he has finished speaking, you may wish to reflect back what you have heard or felt. As we learn to listen to others, so we learn to listen to ourselves and to God.

b) *Speak for yourself.* Own your own issues. Speak only of yourself and about yourself. Describe your experiences in terms of "I", not "we". You need offer to the group only as much about yourself as you feel comfortable in sharing, but be totally honest about what you do share. Allow others to speak for themselves and do not try to do their work for them. The group is there primarily to support people in the work that they have to do.

c) *Focus on the topic.* Avoid "red herrings" and digressions. It is very easy for someone in the group to pick up on a side-issue that a speaker has referred to and so digress from the main topic. For example, in one group a person talked about the loneliness she experienced at boarding school. Another member of the group started to give his views on the advantages and disadvantages of single-sex boarding schools. While this produced an interesting discussion that all the group members could identify with, the speaker felt devalued and quite hurt because the pain of her loneliness "was not heard" by the other members of the group.

d) *No analysis.* The group is not the place for one person to analyse another's problem and practise some amateur psychology! Let each person win his or her own battles. A growth group is not the place for advice giving or intellectual debate. We are there to provide support for each other on the journey to wholeness.

7. **Contribution.** Everyone should be given a chance to contribute. In any group of people there are likely to be some who talk more than others, especially extraverts. This will make introverts inclined to withdraw and leave it to others to do the talking. Everyone is also *free not to contribute* to a particular issue if they do not want to. Respect each other's autonomy and space.

8. **Silence.** Do not be afraid of silence. Some people have an urge to rush in and fill all gaps with talk. Silence can provide an opportunity for people to process what is happening for them. "Speech is silver, silence is golden."

9. **Confidentiality.** Anything said within the group must stay there. Nothing will destroy trust or spoil a growth group more quickly than members talking with others outside about what has been shared in confidence. Solomon said: "A gossip betrays confidence, but a trustworthy man keeps a secret." One of the tasks of the leader or initiator of a group is to ensure that members agree to protect each other's confidentiality.

10. **Prayer.** If all members of the group share a common faith, prayer with and for one another will unite and strengthen a group. But be aware

of the danger of using prayer as a "quick fix" or a way of avoiding pain. Rushing in to pray for people may prevent them from doing the work they need to do themselves.

St Paul's metaphor of the body (1 Corinthians 12:12–31) clearly teaches that we all need each other. The body at work is powerfully demonstrated by a small group that is operating well.

---

### TEN COMMANDMENTS FOR GROWTH GROUPS

1. A commitment to regular attendance
2. Focus on the one speaking, and listen
3. Discussion, but no debate or analysis
4. Clarify, don't evaluate
5. Avoid side-issues
6. Speak only for yourself
7. Win your own battles
8. Appreciate silences
9. Total honesty in all you share
10. Respect group confidentiality

# SCRIPTURE REFERENCES

| | |
|---|---|
| GENESIS | 1:26; 1:27; 2:15; 2:18; 2:24; 3:10; 3:12; 4:3–9; 6:5; 8:21; 9:6; Ch.18. |
| EXODUS | 33:11; Chs. 33, 34. |
| LEVITICUS | 19:18. |
| DEUTERONOMY | 7:6; 7:7, 8; 30:19, 20; 31:21; 32:10. |
| JOSHUA | 24:15. |
| 1 SAMUEL | 20:19. |
| 2 SAMUEL | 12:1–14. |
| 1 CHRONICLES | 28:9; 29:18. |
| JOB | 25:6; Chs. 38–40; 42:7. |
| PSALMS | 8:3–6; 17:8; 22:6; 23:1; 26:2; 34:6, 17; 51:6, 10; 82:6; 103:12; 116:1; 139:2–5; 139:14; 139:15–16; 139:23, 24. |
| PROVERBS | 6:6–11; 9:9; 14:30; 18:9; 20:24, 27; 22:6; 23:7; 31:18–29. |
| SONG OF SOLOMON | 8:6, 7. |
| ISAIAH | 1:18; 26:3; 41:8; 43:1; 43:26; 49:16; 64:2; 65:24. |
| JEREMIAH | 1:5; 17:10; 18:5; 29:12; 31:3; 31:34. |
| MICAH | 7:19. |
| ZECHARIAH | 2:8. |
| MALACHI | 3:17. |
| MATTHEW | 3:17; 5:23, 24; 6:12–15; 6:22; 7:1; 7:7; 9:10–13; 10:30; 11:19; 13:10–13; 13:45, 46; 16:24, 24; 18:22; 19:5; 19:19; 22:37, 38; 22:39; 28:20; Ch.23. |
| MARK | 12:31. |
| LUKE | 1:36–44; 1:56; 2:52; 5:27–32; 7:36–50; 10:27; 10:38–41; 15:1, 2; 15:11–32; 15:31; 18:14; 18:23; 18:29, 30; 19:1–10; 20:47; 22:24; 23:34; 24:13–35. |

| JOHN | 1:14; 1:18; 3:1–21; 4:4–26; 8:1–11; 8:32; 10:3; 10:10; 10:14; 10:34, 35; 12:32; 13:34; 15:3; 15:9; 17:23. |
|---|---|
| ACTS | 2:21; 10:34, 35. |
| ROMANS | 3:23; 4:1–8; 5:3, 4; 5:5; 5:8; 5:10; 7:15, 24; 7:18; 8:1, 2; 8:5–13; 8:15, 23; 8:28; 8:29; 8:39; 12:1; 12:2; 12:3; 12:6–8; 12:15; 13:9; 14:4, 10; 15:7. |
| 1 CORINTHIANS | 2:9; 2:15, 16; 4:3–5; 4:12, 13; 4:16; 6:19, 20; 9:24–27; 11:1; 11:7; 12:1–11; 13:1–3; 13:11; 13:12. |
| 2 CORINTHIANS | 3:18; 4:4; 5:9; 10:4, 5; 12:9, 10. |
| GALATIANS | 1:10; 1:15; 2:20; 3:10–14; 4:5; 4:7; 5:13, 14; 5:19–21; 5:22, 23. |
| EPHESIANS | 1:4–6; 1:11, 18; 2:8, 9; 2:10; 2:19; 3:17–19; 4:13; 4:15; 4:22, 23; 4:28; 4:29; 5:28, 33. |
| PHILIPPIANS | 1:6; 1:10; 2:3; 2:4; 4:11, 12; 4:13. |
| COLOSSIANS | 1:15; 1:21, 22; 1:28; 3:5, 10. |
| 1 THESSALONIANS | 1:3; 1:6, 7; 4:11; 5:11; 5:21. |
| 2 THESSALONIANS | 3:6–13. |
| 2 TIMOTHY | 2:15; 3:2–4. |
| HEBREWS | 1:1, 2; 1:3; 2:6–8; 4:12; 10:25; 12:15; 13:5. |
| JAMES | 1:2–4; 2:8; 2:23; 3:9; 3:5–12. |
| 1 PETER | 2:23; 2:24. |
| 1 JOHN | 1:9; 2:16; 3:1; 4:1; 4:19; 5:14. |
| REVELATION | 12:10; 22:17. |